dac

a memoir

andy onyx

MICRODOT BOOKS

First Printing: 2019

2nd edition 2021

MICRODOT BOOKS

microdot.books@gmail.com

www.andyonyx.co.uk

A CIP catalogue record for this book is available from the British Library

Ordering Information:
Special discounts are available on quantity purchases by corporations, associations, educators, and others. For details, contact the publisher at the above listed address.

ISBN: 9781079101263

Recently a wise person at the BBC decided to upload archived *Man Alive* shows from the late 60s early 70s to iPlayer, so that we might know where we were and where we might be going as a nation today. In amongst the skinheads, gay couples, moody marriages and Hyde Park, there was the story of a young woman who passed away aged just 19, one year into adult life.

She had spent her childhood in the 'care' of the state, for the most part bereft of love or kindness. Her descent took place around Piccadilly, in Eros' shadow, largely unnoticed amidst the carnival of Swinging London until it was too late.

It's my hope, in a still-new century, that such a thing would never be allowed to happen again to a vulnerable young care leaver, here in 'first world' Great Britain or anywhere else. Sometimes hope is all.

Her name was **Gale Parsons** and this book is dedicated to her.

§

innovative and devious methods to divide us. Junking *our* verdant river by throwing in hate and division like rusty bikes and shopping trolleys. They are scapegoating minorities and attacking the 'other' once more: anyone or anything a bit too 'different;' bigot fodder, if you like. Did the countless 'others' in the past not gift us most of the beauty and brilliance that surrounds us today? But we've recently seen the cool breath of technology hiss new life into that 'old trick' once more, forcing the unwanted gift of newer, bluer Meanies on all of us. Very naughty.

Social historians suggest that this as a symptom of tough times, as if prejudice and ignorance (I prefer these terms to the catch all of 'racism') are viruses that lurk silently in the carrier of our society and flare up into sickness when hard times lower our natural immunity - our collective better nature. There is some truth in this theory, like most things, but the strokes are far too broad, even for an old painter like me.

The recollections that follow are true by my own recall. Some names and locations have been changed for the craic, or to let sleeping pups lie, but most haven't. Some of the characters are amalgams but most aren't. There are no war criminals within these pages; we all make mistakes. We can also make better choices too, because there's always a next time. So, let's use it wisely.

Some of what follows doesn't make pretty reading, as with any life it can't always be so, but you won't be spending too much time hiding behind the sofa as there's plenty of love and light along the way also. So, make yourself comfy and I'll get the kettle on…we have lift-off.

1

SEEKER

All of us are born looking up and, with our first cries, the lifelong search for comfort and nourishment begins. If there's a gap beyond the most basic needs, does it really matter? Well, in short when we're without something, anything, it generally matters and sometimes it matters like hell.

As I wrote the word dadless, Microsoft Word underlined it in red and offered 'no suggestions.' I checked against the macabre 'headless,' and got the all clear. As a word it's recognized, accepted and safe 'inside.' With dadless, we are now beyond the confines of the programme. We are going behind the lines…together.

Putting into words my own thoughts and reflections of the historical plight of the many dadless boys and girls out there, I considered the hundreds I've met on my journey who weren't in our position and seemed to be at the centre of happy nuclear families. One in particular stands out from my childhood, Bede, who said that he wished he didn't have a dad. I've known all too many whose fathers, though present, have been judged by their offspring as falling into the oversubscribed category of Crap Dad. We find him mid-table in the league, just above Useless Cunt, but several places above the unspoken, down in the relegation zone, whose crimes and misdemeanours go way beyond the let-downs of their kids. Their mention elicits a quickened heart rate, clenched teeth, a narrowing of the eyes, which then look sideways into the middle-distance, flashing back through the incidents, before a shrug and a return to the safety and control of the present moment.

Within these pages, you will also find several examples of ordinary men, who appeared to have been Dads of Distinction. I witnessed some of their acts of kindness and support. They were like living bonfires in the eldritch night, which I huddled around, shoulder-to-shoulder with their own kids, and enjoyed their light and warmth too, which was a wonderful thing.

We all have skin in this particular game. By virtue of our existence, we've all had fathers, and you may have been blessed with creating them, either with your partner or as your offspring, but is there a distinction between a father and a dad? Or between a biological occurrence and an 18-year duty of care and responsibility? *Dad.* Is it more than a word? It's idealised through absence to the likes of me, a prized title that should be cherished and valued, but what does it mean to them or you? Is it a barbed wire crown or a priceless medal of honour?

The contributor of fifty per cent of my DNA was represented for the majority of my life by a void. The only difference between theories involving Santa Claus and the moon landings is that I'm here, just let me check - yes, correctamundo. *I am here.* Also, there were no other suspects, and the evidence has been an indicator from the off. He contributed the 'dark half.'

My father hailed from Jamaica and was in his mid-thirties when I was born. Some people have an overriding mission or passion which they pursue in adult life, to the exclusion of all other things; his was his career as a professional stage magician. Not for him the life of a frustrated hobbyist, working at the office or factory and doing a 'turn' here and there. He lived and ate by it, travelled the world with it and in a different time. Without what he referred to as 'the colour bar' (in one of our three conversations) he would have achieved much more fame and fortune. He was a decade too old to benefit from the 60s cultural boom, more of a lounge lizard than a flower child, and told me that he'd worked the inherent racism of that era into his act, to the pleasure and amusement of his lighter audience.

My father also had the skills to innovate and exploit his talents, knowledge and intelligence, as an inventor of illusions, much akin to the difference between a pure musician and a songwriter in the music industry. His calling was found as a kid, by gaining the attention and fascination of his own dad when he performed a magic trick for him. He described this as 'Freudian.' Classy bleeder!

Many years later, he performed at a Royal Variety Performance in 1968 (when I was probably in gestation). Top of the bill was the legendary African American all-round entertainer Sammy Davis Junior. At the after-show party, Sammy wanted my father to explain how the trick was done. Like all great illusions, it appeared impossible. My father refused; Sammy became upset. I could imagine his appeals for sacred knowledge including 'brother to brother' and such like. Still my father refused to tell. Consider the doors that could have possibly been opened for him in the industry, on a worldwide scale, by Sammy's endorsement. If he'd only revealed the trick…and broken the most sacred rule of the Magic Circle. On this occasion, he stuck to his principles and creed.

Membership of this organisation must have meant so much to him, that the betrayal was unthinkable, even with a diamond-encrusted carrot being dangled in front of him by the biggest black star on the planet. He saved such betrayals for us expendables, who sprang from the seed he carelessly scattered in his wake. Ours was the cold world outside the Magic Circle, where the wind blew us off the wall, for other kind and selfless souls to pick up our pieces, and stick us back together again, like little brown humpties.

The hard-won success as an illusionist led to him being the first black member of the Inner Magic Circle and a legend within the industry to those in the know. Much later in life, he became a committed family man and faced his responsibilities as a husband and dad to my two other known half-siblings.

One day in 2000, sat at my workstation, I typed his name into a search engine, pressed 'enter' and saw him for the first time in my life. There he was, as I considered then: the architect of my misery, ruiner of lives, donor of DNA, creator of a half-man - fifty per cent blank.

Six months later, I went to my final Glastonbury; this was the last 'fence jump' festival, that was as near as Glastonbury got to Altamont, short of a racist murder by Hell's Angels. There were far too many people, not enough space and lots of bad intentions, creating a very moody vibe. Gangs of lads from the North West, adorned with jester hats and shades, were roaming the site and scanning the crowd for weak prey and easy pickings.

I was with the poet Andrew Walker, who was a special friend and fellow star sailor for a time. We had first met in the early 90s. I had been standing next to the dance floor in the Pier bar in Skegness with my prized purple Jimi Hendrix tee-shirt on. I'd bought it from Selectadisc in Nottingham. He had the exact same one and wandered up and said 'Snap!'

Andrew was a very bright kid, about five years younger than me and still in Grammar School. He stood over six feet tall and resembled a well-fed, young Roger Moore, with the same laid-back, well-spoken charm. Home for him was a lovely detached house called Rivendell in Hagworthingham, part of the hilly countryside area of Lincolnshire known as the Wolds. Indoors were his beautiful flame-haired older sister Zan, two younger half-siblings and a range of rescued pets, including a llama called Lionel. His mum and stepdad, Carol and Denis, who I also regard as beautiful people, were initially concerned about their wayward son making friends with this older 'Rasta' guy in Skegness. I had shoulder length dreadlocks, and at 23, was surely a bad influence, as Andrew was already a gentle rebel dancing to his own tune.

Ten years had passed through thick and thin, mostly thick. Over-indulgence, against all counsel, had taken an axe to the poet's mental health and sadly his travails would recur before the weekend was out.

We were sat by the Carlsberg tent in between the stages, watching the droves of predators and their quarry drift by. Andrew, ever the idealist, was disappointed that I'd jumped the fence for once (along with approx. 50,000 others) as the festival was for a charitable cause. I'd taken the train from Paddington that time; it was a totally different experience from the cross-country pilgrimage drive from Skegness, which I'd undertaken in the previous years.

I'd hit Peak Glasto in 1997, when a 12-strong group of us had all come down in three cars; we had our own significant camp plotted up by the cider bus. The literal high-point being a bonding sortie up on the Green Fields on the Friday night, involving Albert Hoffman, the deity Ganesha, fluorescent puppet shows and the Twelve Tribes of Israel, along with another fellow reveller - Lord Wigam of Irby in the Marsh, my Bewlay Brother. It had all become a little over-familiar since then, and that was my feeble excuse for the fence jump.

Andrew and I had never discussed 'the situation' or my origins at all before, or indeed since that lucid pow-wow in the middle of a million strangers. Our friendship generally revolved around our love of music. Some friends or friendships have theme tunes that stay with you forever. Andrew's was Move on Up by Curtis Mayfield, nothing to do with the NME or the indie fodder of the day. It was on a mix tape that he was playing in our car as we pulled into the Phoenix Festival a couple of years before. Thinking of Andrew now, I hear the horns and frantic conga beats of that track, and feel the anticipation and excitement again of what the coming weekend would reveal. That's his tune, upbeat and optimistic, not the sad reflective Shine on You Crazy Diamond by Pink Floyd, that depicted both his and Syd Barrett's[3] fate.

There in the Glastonbury dust, at the imaginary convergence of ancient ley lines, Andrew sat and listened intently as I spilled the beans. He was given a precursor of the situation and the emotional fallout that ensued. I'd gone over the moment of revelation that unfolded before my eyes: the pre-broadband modem had started up like an electronic pantomime

---

[3] Syd (Roger) Barret 1946-2006, founder member, lead singer and creative lynch pin of (The) Pink Floyd left the band in 1968 due to psychosis speculated to have been triggered by excessive use of psychedelic drugs.

donkey - *Eee Awww schhhhhhh* - I'd clicked the link and slowly from the top, block by block, pixel by pixel, the culprit was revealed. There. In full colour and character. It was a publicity photo of him in lounge lizard garb, a debonair black man levitating a giant deck of cards. Big hands - check, high forehead - check. Hang on, thank Christ I don't have those ears! The weight that came off my shoulders as I sat glued to the screen was beyond description.

I'd got it all off my chest in the time it took us to sink our paper cup pints in the Solstice sun. At the conclusion, my eyes and head were down. I felt Andrew's large hand on my shoulder.

'Now I know what's been holding you back,' he smiled.

We then got to our feet and got on with Glastonbury.

The revelation begged the question that had never been asked: how could I have led a normal existence, with normal pastimes, relationships and aspirations, when I had a visual blank for fifty per cent of my DNA, the fifty per cent that made me so different from my peers for 33 years, at that? Andrew was right. It was all special: moment, friend, time and place, and I had an answer to match. It was simple…. I couldn't. But I now had to get my head around the once in a lifetime unmasking. It wasn't exactly a Luke Skywalker moment as I still had both hands and actually knew who my father was. Nonetheless, putting a face to the absent but present was mind-blowing.

I had been warned by Mum, since I realised I was dadless, that my father had been an older man when I was born. She told me he was married and would have no interest in me. This was partly to shield me from disappointment and also to keep the waters clear as,

11

although everyone in the family had got on with their lives, the emotional scar tissue was delicate, and the old wounds of 'the situation' could be very easily re-opened. I decided that if or when I finally married, and felt good about myself, especially if fatherhood beckoned, that would be the right time, with the blessing of my wife, to try to make contact. That would happen in time, five years' time to be exact.

Along with the online article I had seen that day was a local BBC piece of my father performing for a local school, as the Magic Story Teller. He was now retired but also working as a hypnotist in Nottingham. Since the late 80s he'd been two hours away from where he'd dumped his DNA back in 1968. Could he have possibly avoided taking his new family for a day out to the seaside for fifteen years? That would take a lot of excuses beyond the weather. Could the bitter, dadless cynic in me back then be forgiven for asking if the hypnotism, like charity had begun at home?

2

THE SITUATION

I'll try to make clear the important points of my beginnings and what I've referred to as 'the situation.'

I couldn't stay with my mother; the nurses had recognised that despite the fact I had big green eyes I was what they called back then, half-caste. Mixed heritage in today's definition.

Prior to 'the situation,' my mother had proven herself to be what she was: an intelligent and self-possessed young woman. A doer, not talker or dreamer. She had decided to join up and serve in the RAF, and her life was going in the right direction under her own steam, with no obvious advantages of birth or circumstances to draw on. She emerged from the relatively catastrophic event of 'the situation' that followed to enjoy a long and happy marriage to a good man, motherhood to my two half-sisters and later a successful career. She was a part of my life and supported me from a distance as much as 'the situation' would allow.

All the ins and outs of what happened and the more personal aspects of 'the situation' aren't for now, but after some pinball involving the Catholic church, late 1960's Social Services, and some well-meaning but doomed intentions, I wound up where I should have gone straight away, with my grandparents.

Social Services had advised that placement in a city would be wiser, as 'coloured people' were more prevalent, and I wouldn't be alienated or stand out as much compared to the small seaside town of Skegness in Lincolnshire, which was where my mother's family hailed from. Thankfully, my grandparents were well up for it, although coming back to dirty nappies and all the rest must have been a blow for them, or more rightly my grandma. Although she had plenty of practice, having raised five kids after the war virtually single-handed. Her youngest son was 21 and serving overseas with the army.

As a young man my grandad, the original Mick O'Connor, had opted for a short life and a merry one. He was the oldest of his siblings and raised in the Cabra area of Dublin in a family of fairground people or non-gypsy showmen, if you like. He'd wound up in Skegness before the war due to my Great-Granny O'Dowd-O'Connor calling in a favour from a young showman/entrepreneur she'd met on the fairgrounds in Ireland, who was planning a new holiday camp on the site of his static fairground in Ingoldmells. His name was Billy Butlin.

It was there that he met my grandma, Betty. He subverted the usual chat-up methods by grabbing her handbag and half-heartedly running off to be chased and apprehended by her, and the rest, as they say, was history. After a whirlwind romance, he proposed by dangling her off the mini bridge on the seafront waterway; she gave him a thick ear for his trouble. They'd married a short time after, started what would become a large family and that was it.

In late middle-age, Grandad's health karma was on the march. He'd spent decades of summer seasons working as a Wrates Photographer, resplendent in candy-striped jacket, straw boater hat and the occasional prop of a monkey on his shoulder. His patch was on the seafront promenade, and he'd captured the happy times of generations of the same families on their summer holidays. The invite would be there from the dads of these families for a drink in the Hildred's pub in the evening, and Grandad was always willing to oblige without too much twisting of his arm.

It's said that the world's first spaceman, Colonel Yuri Gagarin, never paid for a drink again after returning to Earth, a trifle of expense to the benefactors to keep his glass full in exchange for the honour of his company. It invited dependency. The personal cost was much more than standing a thousand rounds of drinks. It was paid publicly by the likes of Gagarin, the legendary footballer George Best and thousands of other celebs, and in private by hedonistas, nobodies and a talented seafront photographer of no great renown.

By the time I showed up, Grandad's years of dedication to his chosen path had led to a shot heart, and regular admission to the village hospital. He wasn't around for much longer after I went to Tennyson Green. So, over the next umpteen years, I was brought up by my grandma, who I always called Mum. Adoption wasn't allowed back then for people of a certain age, so Mum was officially my full-time long-term foster parent. As the events unfold, hopefully the reasons for the capital 'M' become apparent to the reader.

3

TENNYSON GREEN FOREVER

Head east from Nottingham to just above the pointy bit on the map, and don't stop until your feet get wet! Then you will most likely be on Skegness beach. Probably the spot where Kevin Costner's Robin Hood landed in his boat, returning from the crusades in the movie Prince of Thieves, before riding on horseback five minutes to Sherwood Forest -Yeah, right!

'Skegness is so Bracing,' is the tag-line of the town's mascot, the Jolly Fisherman. The historic image of him running on the sand, arms outstretched, greets you by the roadside as if you enter the town. He's always appealed to the city dwellers to come and grab some sun, sea air, and fun, and, of course, spend their hard-earned cash doing so. The area inland from the Wash on the east coast of Lincolnshire was first claimed by a Viking invader, Skeggi -The Bearded One, who named it after himself, as was the tradition. Centuries later, the town began to develop tourism. Carried on the crest of the Industrial Revolution's wave, coastal areas became seaside resorts around Britain in the late 1800s, including Brighton, Blackpool, Margate, Morecombe and, of course, Skegness, serving their respective regions.

As a resort, the town was largely patronised as a holiday destination by the factory and pit workers of the East Midlands and South Yorkshire. This lasted from the 1890s until the mid-1980s when the miners and their communities endured a long strike, the loss of which spelt the demise of the British Coal Industry. Holidays abroad became popular and affordable for the following generations; the week-long hotel breaks in Skeggy, which their grandparents had enjoyed, evolved into overnights, day trips and weekend caravan stays.

In the good times, youth cults also flocked to the seaside at Bank Holidays from the mid-60s onwards: mods, rockers, skinheads, greasers and punks, evolving first into the casuals then ravers. The older generation may equate the town with the original Butlins Camp, a game-changer providing affordable holidays with built-in entertainment for Britain's working-class families of the 50s and beyond. The younger generation reminisce about the Pleasure Dome, also in Ingoldmells, which was a mecca for the ravers of the 1990s, the east coast's microscopic answer to Liverpool's Cream.

In the early 1970s, where my story picks up, a summer season ran from Easter to September, when the kids went back to school. Following this, life would go on for the locals, but the town would go into semi-hibernation from October to March, with the seasonal traders having to live off their takings for that period. They'd then revive like sleepy hungry bears for the upcoming Easter, when it would all begin again.

If you come out of the train station, turn right, take the first left and next right, you'll be there. Tennyson Green. I've recently been told of a Nigerian saying that it takes a village to raise a child. Well, that makes The Green the little village that raised me, along with Mum, in those formative years. It was my sanctuary, magical idyll and safe haven from the last falling debris of 'the situation.' The Green is about a mile from the sea, which you can hear roaring when the tide is in, and smell the salt air carried on the breeze...

A week in my life, 1972 (memory wakes):

I hear the coo-coo of wood pigeons and see a line of daylight streaming through above the curtains across the ceiling. Pink and blue fluffy kittens are on the mattress in my cot. I try to grab them, but I can't. Then I realise ... It's because they're only pictures, but they're lovely ... you can't always get what you want, and you can't always touch what you see. These were my first memories. Maybe my very first disappointment, but life goes on
...

Our house, number 27, has an arched passageway that divides it from next door and links the front and back garden. I drive my red plastic peddle car between the two areas of my little universe. Ouch. I'm growing, and my shins are scraping on the front beneath the white steering wheel. I'm becoming a bigger boy.

I go everywhere with Mum. The weekly routine includes the trip to Mrs Maples, the hairdresser, which is nice. It's warm and smells nice too. I'm given UFO and Joe 90 toys to play with on the floor, and the ladies are friendly and say hello.

We go to the library also. It's OK but I must be quiet and keep still.

Then on to the shops. In the lift at the Co-op it's my job, like Midge, to press the button, which lights up red. There are also yellow and green pointed lights at floor level which are hot to the touch and intrigue me.

In the shops the girls at the till often make a fuss, along the lines of, 'Ohhh, isn't he lovely.' All a bit embarrassing. 'Ohhh, are you shy?' No. Just mildly embarrassed.

We take a longer journey to where the monkey puzzle tree is next to a church. There are always birds singing and the off-sweet scent of decaying flowers. Mum brings new ones (for Grandad).

Not a bad routine in my push buggy, which I call Chitty Chitty Bang Bang because Mum pulls the canopy down when it rains. Soon I grow out of it and have to walk everywhere. It's a bit of a drag on foot, as is this growing lark, generally. The downside of becoming a bigger boy is offset by starting at the Play School on Algitha Road, which breaks the routine up, for me and Mum. One of the ladies is very nasty, but when Mum comes to collect me, she's very nice, which is confusing. Welcome to deception. There's lots of playing in the sandpit and singing songs like I Hear Thunder and Incey Wincey Spider. I don't like spiders. Life beyond our garden is a doddle (for now...)

The Green was built as council housing after the Second World War. Mum, her four siblings, who were then in their teens, Nan (Mum's mum), and a nutty whippet dog called Prince, who thought he was human, transferred there from Spirewick Avenue on the other side of town in the early 60s.

It's a hexagonal estate of two-storey terraced houses with an internal road that wraps round a disc of grass about 50 metres in diameter, which was enveloped by a hedgerow. Full-grown beech trees stood at intervals around the edges, punctuated by a horse chestnut tree at one end and a tall, elegant silver birch at the entrance.

The trees were way too large to climb, except for by the big boys like Chipper Pearce, my friend Lulu's oldest brother. The chestnut tree was right outside their house. In the autumn, Chipper would scale the tree with ease and jump up and down on the branches, bringing conkers raining down, to our delight. There were small fledgling trees also in protective cages at low level.

From the age of four, pre-school, I could play out on the Green with the other kids. It's unthinkable today but the threat of a stranger lurking nearby wasn't as significant back then, as it is now. It's true about doors being open, babies left with neighbours and the community protecting itself. But there was a threat of sorts from bigger boys. Boys who would cast a dark and scary shadow: the Wagstaffs, Bingo, Gary Munter, and Roy Pugson. Between them, they would punctuate the joy, friendship and protection I enjoyed on the Green, with abject fear and misery.

The Wagstaffs seemed to be almost as big as the trees. They had long blond hair, massive flared trousers and chunky boots. They had the opposite opinion of me to the girls behind the tills in town. For me, they were seriously bad news. They'd throw stones from a distance and spit at me once they were in range.

They introduced me to the names and words that I didn't at first understand, but they made sure I could repeat them and sent me indoors to tell them to Mum.

These boys had the dubious honour of being the very first of a long line to make me clearly aware that I was different. In time, the hedgerow around the Green would be removed as the council turned the central area into a car park, and a little later most of the other trees would be seen off by Dutch Elm disease and reduced to stumps, leaving the silver birch and conker tree as the last survivors. Mum was relieved when the hedge went, because at least she could see what I was doing and what was happening, instead of me being hidden from view and running indoors in tears.

After my introduction to the Wagstaffs, and the enlightenment they'd granted me, I'd shoot indoors at the first sight of them approaching in the distance. This was very frightening if I was at the far side of the Green and spotted them late. I had to run toward them and hope I got to the gate before they noticed me. A David Attenborough voice-over would have been apt as the predator Wags hunted and chased me, their quarry. They provided my little, four-year-old ticker with its initial sharp bursts of adrenaline and probably my first grey hairs: nowadays described as the fight or flight response. It was definitely flight for little Andrew then. The fight would come in due course, but much later...

Back then, our family unit, in addition to me, was Mum, Nan, (my great grandmother, who lived in the back room) and Brian, my uncle. He'd come back aged 21 from the army following Grandad's passing. He was the crucial male influence in my life, over six feet tall and resembling both a Pepper-era Paul McCartney and John Cleese. Brian had a lot of time for me and regarded me as his younger brother. Always an assertive and aggressive character, if he caught sight of my tormentors in the act he'd be outside like a flash. In one instance, a kid off Sandbeck Avenue, Dougie, pulled a knife on me. There was an immediate intervention, and it was dealt with.

I bumped into Dougie, 25 or so years later, on the

street outside my flat on Algitha Road. He remembered the incident after all that time and we discussed it for a minute or two, but Dougie remained indignant. I let it go, as I was way beyond settling childhood scores with my fists by then. Dougie never quite became a model citizen; he had recently been seen on national TV in CCTV footage, breaking into a chemist with his toddler under his arm. Nature or nurture? Who will ever know?

To counter the darkness of the Wagstaffs and co I had 'sunbeams' like the girls next door. Gaye, the oldest, was sensible and a bit distant but Angela, and Nicola were my pals, along with Lulu and Mandy from across The Green. My tightest mate was Andy Gowling on the other side, but he could be led astray by Chris Jones in the corner house. Chris was a couple of years older and wayward with a dominant personality. I'd class him as a frenemy (a combination of friend and enemy) depending on which way the wind was blowing.

Bingo was from the other corner house and was another rotter, not quite as big and bad as the Wagstaffs but a 'mare just the same. In between me getting my first beloved bike with stabilisers and riding around the Green to my heart's content, one of my favourite pastimes was standing on the gate and watching the clouds and the world drift by. One of that bleeder Bingo's favourite tricks was to ride past on his bike and gob in my direction, until the issue was raised over at his house and he was 'educated' by his older sister Annie. He would have been just a kid of ten or eleven himself then and needed straightening out. Annie must have done a good job. The strange fact is that, unlike Dougie, Bingo did grow up to be an all-round good egg and pillar of the community.

Further around the Green from Lulu, were

teenage siblings Diane and Stuart. They'd take me out a lot of the time and I received all Stuart's old action men. They were the originals, before the evolution of fuzzy hair, eagle eyes and gripping hands. One of which has somehow followed me around to this day. Their parents kept budgerigars in a large cage in the back garden, just near the passage. The little birds were vivid reds, yellows, blues and greens and fascinated me, to the point that I'd go through the passage to the back garden unaccompanied, much to Mrs Baker's consternation and amusement.

'Andrew, what are you doing there?' she'd say.

'Looking at the budgies,' I replied with a child's simple logic.

Our next-door neighbours on the other side were an old couple, the Moyers, with their pet tabby cats, Ting-a-Ling and Tiny Fellow. They were big animal welfare supporters, and Mrs Moyer also made and distributed lovely cakes, which were very popular with us lot. Mr Moyer was a Scotsman and an archery enthusiast. A few years later, he gave me my first bow and a handful of arrows as an unexpected gift, which was very kind. He had a large straw target at the end of his garden which he'd shoot at with a cross bow. I'd often hear a click followed by a thud a millisecond later as he practised.

In addition to the council tearing down the hedge and creating the car park, they also developed back roads to the houses by cutting our long, lovely gardens in half. The Green was suddenly dominated by mountains of mud, clay, concrete and water, asking to be played in, way before the advent of Health and Safety. It was truly slugs, snails and puppy dogs' tails stuff for the kids in the area.

For that period, I went out to play clean and came back, without fail, covered in mud with my wellies full of water, lapping on to the floor.

'Oh Andrew! You mucky pup!' was Mum's general response when she saw me at the back door. I remember exclaiming, 'Mum, it's just impossible, no matter what I do I can't stay clean!'

Next stop: I'm standing in the kitchen sink getting hosed down, much too mucky for the bath.

By now, the threat from the biggest boys had, for the most part, gone. They'd either moved away, been kicked into touch or got to the point that they didn't bother with little kids anymore. Could Mr Moyer's crossbow had been put to some macabre use? I still had to deal with Pugson and Munter though; they were nearer my age, so they couldn't be avoided. Playing on the back road put me more or less in their territory and I'd be told, 'Get down your own end!' by grown-ups when spotted around there. When my tormentors started stronging it on the Green, our grown-ups would give them the same. So, it was a bit of cat and mouse as the years ticked by. I was definitely the mouse.

I believe the stick I got from that lot, and the cruel aggressive little blighters I met at infant school, had a subtle but obvious effect on my mental health. Something, thanks to the revelations of the young Royals and others in the public eye, we can talk about now without the risk of shame or ridicule, hopefully.

I developed something that was called at the time a 'food fad.' I don't remember having an appetite until I was 12 years old and would only, according to Mum, eat 'sweet stuff'. Mealtimes were murder at school. OK, school dinners in the early 70s weren't up to Michelin Star quality but that didn't stop the others wolfing them down; a dustbin lid would have suited some kids, sadly and almost literally in the case of one.

I'd sit there with a plate full of whatever and

point-blank refuse to eat. They'd tried holding me there alone in the dinner hall with a cold plate in front of me until I ate it. That tactic was time-bound, so it was an obvious failure as after playtime I'd be missed in class and someone had to take me there, most often a severely pissed-off dinner lady. This only compounded the isolation and humiliation.

The school contacted Mum, and it was agreed between them that I wasn't to eat my Wagon Wheel with my milk (pre-Milk Snatcher Thatcher) at break time, as a means of increasing my appetite. Again, it didn't work. In these early years, there were many dinnertime rows and tears with my extended family whenever I stayed somewhere else. The only feeling I had in the pit of my stomach as dinnertime approached was an overwhelming dread as I anticipated the forthcoming clash. This was upsetting on so many levels for my family. There was the insult of good food that had been prepared with care being rejected and wasted, as well as the financial aspect. They were from the rationed generation, who spent their childhoods always starving, and here was Andrew refusing to eat, only wanting 'sweet stuff.'

I wasn't the only one around with problems. Converse to me at school there was a boy called Kean, who had a squinted eye and was never clean. He was so hungry all the time that he picked up and ate crisps that had been dropped on the ground in the school yard. Another, Ryan, had what they called then a 'club foot' in a black stirrup boot, probably from contracting polio. Everyone's shins got acquainted with Ryan's boot if they crossed him in any way. We were all afraid of him. He popped up again many years later in secondary school. He hadn't developed properly and seemed small and pale compared to the rest of us, almost like Tiny Tim from A Christmas

Carol. His aggression had also diminished; he wasn't kicking anyone anymore.

In recent years, psychologists have related the craving of sugar to the relief of stress or as a comforter following a bitter experience. I believe the 'food fad' was just that, a manifestation of the deep upset of my experiences and alienation. The first but far from last blip in my mental health. As a child on the receiving end, I'd deeply internalised the pain. What would now be called an eating disorder. Visible self-harm or destructive acts may or may not be easier to notice; that's if anyone is looking. Even then, who knows what to do?

Mum had taken me to the doctors with the problem, and they'd had little interest past the cursory advice:

'Don't worry too much, he'll grow out of it.'

In time I did, after much heartache for all concerned. Come adolescence, by some degree of luck and support, it was over. Physical work on the boating lake and martial arts filled the void, soothed the pain and gave me self-worth, self-respect and at last a healthy appetite and balanced diet. I hope there is the support to look a little deeper into the root causes when eating disorders manifest in children today. There is no cotton wool solution, because the exposure to trauma has taken place. Whether the child is dadless, or suffering any kind of trauma or abuse, can we undo what's done? Maybe not but if we can look a little deeper at the cause, as another song says '…then we can start …to make it better.'

4

KUNG FU and CLANGERS

It has been said, here and there, that the 70s was the children's decade. All things in relativity, which isn't? From my perspective as a child in the UK at that time, there was certainly a world of our own to inhabit, supported by the fact that most, not all, homes had a colour TV. Mum rented ours from the Co-op and thank God she did. I'd begun to realise that I was dadless for the first time around then, but if the choice was given between having a dad or a colour TV, it wouldn't have been a hard one for me, but neither would the choice between a Curly Wurly[4] or a slap-up Sunday lunch.

Those that were involved in the creative side of children's TV had been on the receiving end of the cultural explosion of the arts in the mid to late 60s. It must have been great to be in art or film school in that era. The art students had become working grown-ups and parents themselves. They vented the output of colour and imagination to their offspring, my generation. This reached us through the TV screen, on a Saturday morning and an hour or so at teatimes in the week. There was no 'catch up,' 'on demand' or 24-hour channels back then. It was strictly rationed in short windows of time through the one and only TV,

---

[4] Curly Wurly- a 1970's lattice toffee-covered chocolate bar

and the whole family would be exposed together. It's hard to imagine a comparison today with those TV events like Top of the Pops that would be discussed amongst the whole population the following day. So, for me and my young peers, daily life was immersed in highly imaginative and, what we would realise many years later, somewhat hallucinogenic creations: The Magic Roundabout, Wombles, Banana Splits, Fingerbobs, Mr Benn and the wonderful worlds of Postgate & Firmin, including the Clangers, as well as the tea time science fantasy of Dr Who, the Six Million Dollar Man, the Tomorrow People and Planet of the Apes.

At Cavendish Road Infants School, part of the playground ritual was a, 'Who wants to play (fill in the blank)?' This started with two or three of us with linked arms across the shoulders. The line would grow as a revolving procession on either side with the recruits continuing the chant. This was possibly the first experience in our seven-to-nine-year-old lives of arriving at a democratic decision!

'Who wants to play Planet of the Apes?'

This was a regular winner and always well-subscribed. The standard blue or red (non-branded) tracksuit with two white stripes on the sleeves and outside legs was all the rage then. Mine was red and I loved it, just as much as Emily loved Bagpuss[5]. I was very disappointed as the sleeves seemed to shorten as I grew. Enough empty crisp packets had been saved to get free gifts of iron-on patches, a V peace sign in

[5] Bagpuss - mid 70s stop motion animated TV series by Small Films duo of Oliver Postgate (animation and narrator) and Peter Firmin (sets, props and illustration). Bagpuss was an old grey woollen cloth cat. It would come to life and colour each episode after a spell by his owner, Emily Firmin, Peter's daughter.

Stars and Stripes and an S. Neither me nor Mum realised it was the Superman symbol and she sewed it on upside down, bless her.

Going to school in my red tracksuit top would elicit a special bonus come playtime. When we elected to play Planet of the Apes, the tracksuit would allow you innocent segregation into the special, desirable elite of the pursued human astronauts or simply 'humans,' not an unpleasant memory but this did stick in my mind. These differences, experiences and preferences forming at this early age were defining our personalities, and who we were becoming, at school and at home.

Maybe sexual awakening is simply realising who you're looking at and how you feel. It came to me around that time but not, I must stress, in a carnal sense. Just a 'I can't stop looking at Jackie (or Jack) Lamp-Post and it makes my chest and tummy feel funny' kind of thing; crushes, if you like. Jackie, I thought, was the loveliest looking thing ever, but she wasn't having any of it, no sir; she was a pint-sized Aunt Sally. But then I met Zara…. Bosh! She had a heart-shaped face, and big blue expressive eyes. I was in love, as far as I knew, totally sold. She even had the same name as another Zara(h) who I also adored on Saturday teatimes, Dr Who's assistant! Our feelings were mutual as far as I was concerned, and I lived for the playtimes. She was my favourite thing, sod 'Who wants to play.' I even introduced her to Mum when she collected me at home time. Then the interloper appeared. Zara's head was turned; maybe she was easily bored. She was playing with David Thornett, not me. Rejection! I looked at her. I looked at him. I couldn't work it out, but it felt bad, very bad.

Here was an introduction to the perpetual harsh realities of the love triangle (sadly not the last). Maybe

I cried. She soon came back to me and gave David the elbow. But following the summer break, I would be going to a new school around the corner from home, Richmond Drive, and wouldn't see her again, or so I thought. Zara made a big imprint on my tiny mind. I had eyes for no other.

I could even see her likeness in the big-eyed queen of hearts from the standard deck of playing cards! I never forgot her in the following years and would sometimes ride my bike to that part of the town, as if behind enemy lines, to see if I could catch a furtive glimpse. I carried a tiny torch and we would be re-united in secondary school, some four years later.

Also, in that mix of Zara, TV, playtime, home life, reality and imagination, was something that stood alone but would return to significance again and again, as I grew in awareness from child to adolescent, through to adulthood and the present. Its basis, originator and underpinning content would go on to fill the dadless void and soothe the emptiness and alienation in the decades to come. This was another Saturday afternoon programme, which I understood much less than the previous mentioned shows, and would only have viewed in passing first time, drawn in by the Wild West setting. It was both fascinating but mystifying to an eight-year-old. 'Why don't they have hair?' 'What is China?' 'What is a grasshopper?' And many more questions than answers.

It was called Kung Fu.

5

AN ACT OF ABJECT
COWARDICE

The new school on Richmond Drive, around
the corner from us at Tennyson Green, was a
big deal. A brand-new modern construction
on open fields. The general understanding was that
the school would service the families from the 'nice'
part of town. Those that owned shops and seasonal
businesses and populated the streets and avenues off
and around Drummond Road, up to the exclusive
Seacroft area.

Until then, they would have had to go to the
County Junior on Brunswick Drive, near to the
Cavendish Road Infant School. The kids and families
like us from the council estates in close proximity to
the new school were like little flies in the ointment and
wouldn't have been considered in the planning. From
the moment I stepped in, I felt like a pauper. (You've
done love triangle, young sir, how about a taste of
inferiority? Plant deeply, feed regularly and you'll be
blessed with a lovely king-sized sherbet in years to
come! Sherbet dip, chip on your shoulder-remember?)

Mum explained, years later following my
academic decline, that there was a choice of schools
between the new and the established, but she believed,
with the best of intentions, that the new school would

have the best opportunities and fresh, enthusiastic teachers.

The headmistress, Miss Rhydes, did not fit that template at all. She was in her 60s, an authoritarian heavy smoker with rusty, 'English' teeth and, judging by her hair style, she was also clearly a Maggie fan. The Tory party leader, Margaret Thatcher, was the new flavour and all the rage with the target audience of the new school. To them, she was the best thing since sliced bread; manna from heaven.

Later, I learnt that Maggie was behind the milk disappearing that we used to so enjoy, and which also sustained me through my food fad in those early years. She was dubbed Milk-Snatcher Thatcher by the press. Soon Maggie would introduce 'right to buy,' enabling council tenants to own their home. We, as a family, bought our council house years later, when she was selling England by the pound, so we benefitted, but what about the next generations? Maggie somehow forgot to spend much of the proceeds on new social housing.

The Richmond Drive school was a ten-minute walk, but that was the only advantage. I was incarcerated there until after the 11+. The teaching staff there naturally seemed old to me at the time, but I guess they would have been around 23 in most instances and fresh out of the universities or polytechnics of the big cities. They would have been familiar with other ethnicities - more so than older teachers or the parents of the target audience. I don't know what they thought of me.

Mum said that the parent's evenings were excruciating as she waited in line to see the teachers, who were fawning over the seemingly prosperous younger parents: jewellers, police, the manager of M&S etc. and giving her short shrift as she explained to them that she was my grandmother. 'Oh, err…. yes, Andrew, er… let me see….'

(Written off again and again, no hope, not a prayer: the blessing of we, the anti-fragile.)

By nine or ten years of age, I had a long understanding that I was completely different to everyone else and couldn't hide it. Black people were bestowed with a flattering array of 'names' in the UK back then, which I will list for the uninitiated. It could be argued that there are many more 'names' than you find for other ethnic groups or minorities, which in general, have two or three (with the exception of the LGBTQ community who have historically received the same degree of contempt). So here goes: nigger, coon, black jack, sambo, chocolate drop, nig-nog, sooty, blacky, golliwog, darky, pickaninny (Boris' favourite) and, of course, jungle bunny, the jungle being the place which I was told that I should 'get back to,' by those enlightened souls who thought that Tarzan was Africa and Africa was Tarzan.

As little kids, my cousin Math and I would be referred to in gentle banter as Tarzan and Jai, which we happily embraced. He was four months older and seemed to be a third taller than me (to this day) with ash blonde 'Milky Bar Kid' hair.

At least I wasn't called Cheetah! The comparison was based on the early 70s Ron Ely version of TV Tarzan (Donald Trump stole his haircut). This Tarzan was no Lord Greystoke raised by apes, but was an educated, athletic, hippy. He could handle himself in a scrap and had opted for jungle life instead of 'civilisation,' intermingling with local tribes and the wildlife with ease and fighting the bad guys bare foot.

'Hippy Tarzan' had a paternal relationship with a little dark-skinned boy, Jai, and his pet chimpanzee, Cheetah, completed the happy trio. Tarzan often carried Jai in one arm and the chimp in the other. Did they all live happily together in a treehouse up a Yew Tree? Looking back, it all seemed entirely innocent, though Jane was conspicuous in her absence, so Tarzan was out there on his own, as a single foster parent.

When it comes to each derogatory 'name,' could we say there is a spiky scale of offence for one in comparison to another? Aside from the Jai tag, which I took as a compliment, early on they all hurt more than any stick or stone. I didn't read them as a child. I was called most of them, on a regular basis. In my world, they were aimed at me and only me; there was no black community, as in Brixton or Toxteth. Who called me them? Very few kids and a couple of adults, but this happened often, and until my adolescence I couldn't get too confident or loud or I'd be brutally reminded by someone of my obvious difference. By adolescence, the powder keg was full, the David Banner[6] moment would come to pass. More on that later …

The majority of those listed 'names,' I found out decades later, were regularly broadcasted on a TV programme called Love thy Neighbour. I'd never seen it; I'd have been in bed by the time it was on, as would most of my peers. The scripted language is so inflammatory that it isn't likely to be broadcast on terrestrial TV again. The premise of the show was that two couples, black and white, are next door neighbours. The wives get along and are friends but there is a state of hostility between the husbands, based on race. The white protagonist used most of

---

[6] Dr David Banner (Bill Bixby) the main protagonist from the TV series The Incredible Hulk. Following a gamma radiation overdose, Banner transforms into the Hulk when he loses the plot with extreme stress.

those 'names' I listed above; the black man was generally restricted to the words, snowflake and honky.

Yes, as with Alf Garnett, the ultimate joke was always on the ignorant white man, but this was generally lost on the likes of him sat in front of the TV. In this era, it was widely accepted, globally, that a black man was 'less' and nowhere near equal, which possibly accounts for the amount of 'names' attributed. The hateful dialogue would have been repeated day to day at home by some of the parents of my peers, most likely their dads and aimed at the likes of Great Britons like Derrick Griffiths, Floella Benjamin, Trevor MacDonald and Viv Anderson as they were beamed through 'the idiots' lantern' into living rooms across the land, on Play School, News at Ten and Match of the Day respectively. It was passed like a virus from parents to children, father to son. The learnt behaviour incubated in its hosts, only to flare up and manifest again in the school yard or dinner queue. 'That's m'boy!'

The message was that black people didn't belong here in the UK, Europe and even in the USA; the black man was bereft of any status beyond his community. They belong somewhere else and should go back. They, like other immigrants, especially including the Irish in the UK back then, were fair game and the butt of any joke.

A popular part of the 70s cockney comedian Jim Davidson's act, were stories about his wide-eyed mate Chalky, with the bass Jamaican accent and the falsetto laugh. But remember, it was OK because he made it crystal clear to all of us that Chalky was his mate. Jim wasn't displaying his intellect by painting 'niger go howm' on Chalky's wall in white emulsion. To be fair to Jim, he gave it to everybody back then, even

'Babylon' - the police force. But the police are an institution. Chalky was one man and everyone was laughing at him not with him. Including the police ...

Beyond name-calling, I'd become aware of the existence of something called the National Front, maybe through the occasional party political broadcast on TV, or by hearsay from other kids. The skinhead revival had begun off the back of punk, and an article on 'Paki bashing' had been in the red-top papers. This prompted one skinhead to politely ask me if I was one. Math and I always said, take anyone, a hippy for example, skin them and put them in the uniform they look frightening, but it doesn't actually make them harder. The main thing I understood was that the NF hated black people. I knew very well the way people communicated their dislike of my colour as individuals, never mind as an organised group of adults. The thought of that terrified me.

One of the kids, Dwayne, who I'd never had any issue with before, piped up one day that his dad was in the National Front. He was an average kid, maybe a little smaller in stature than most of us. He had two younger brothers who were miniature Russian doll-like versions of him: pale, freckled with jet-black pudding bowl/Mr Spock haircuts and identical clothes. He had come from a place faraway called 'Sarfend.'

We got on generally, but without thought one day I blurted a comparison between the NF and a particular farmyard animal. Things moved on; the subject changed, and I thought no more about it. I'd receive a similar cutting remark many years later about my grandfather, from a nasty old man who should have known better. But it's in the job description of ten-year-old boys to make insensitive, uncalled-for, out-of-line, comments to their peers, *modus operandi*, especially for dadless ones like me.

All was forgotten until one evening leaving school, walking up the drive to the gates, I was confronted by a lady. She jabbed a sharp manicured finger at my chest. It stopped just short. 'You!' she said through clenched teeth.

'Huh!?'

'You! You said Dwayne's dad was a farmyard animal.'

I took a backward step. 'What?'

She repeated the accusation.

I looked behind her. Life was proceeding as normal with everyone filtering away from the school gates on their way home.

'No, I didn't.'

'Yes, you did,' she shot back and stepped forward.

Then to the side, by the bike sheds, I saw Dwayne; he was pale and tearful. His younger brothers were there with no comprehension of what was going on. They were either side of a man standing tall, arms folded with a big grin on his face topped with Mr Spock hair. Dwayne's dad.

Jab! 'Apologise!' she hissed.

Again, I looked past them; the crowd had almost gone. Where are the teachers? No one's noticed what's going on and I'm rooted to the spot.

'I didn't say that. I said it about the NF,' I stammered.

Jab. 'APOLOGISE!' Now a shout. She was escalating.

There I was, 9.5 years old with these people in front of me and completely alone. If I had the front to shout, 'Fuck you!' what could they have done? Would she have got away with assaulting me, as we were virtually alone now? If I had the strength to say nothing and stand my ground, what then? Maybe an expletive tirade from her with most, if not all, of the 'names' listed above. As it was, to no shame, I caved in.

'OK, I'm sorry,' I said.

'You'd better be,' she snapped and walked back to her family and off they all went, home for tea. Was this lady a proud victorious lioness, protecting the honour of her cub and pride or the perpetrator, complicit with her husband? Or had it been an act of abject cowardice?

How long had they cased me out to make sure I was alone? If even Math was with me, he would have told them where to go, no probs, never mind my uncles Brian or Mick. But the approach came specifically because they caught me on my own. If they had any bottle, why not come to the house? Too risky? Could there be some comeback from a grown man or even an old lady? As angry as I was that there was no protection for me, I felt for Dwayne, standing there by the bike sheds. He just been force fed a noxious cocktail of shame, familial embarrassment, emasculation and humiliation - down in one.

It was around the time of this incident that something else happened, which, at the time of writing, I have only just linked. I made the decision to walk out of school. I left before the end of playtime and walked out the gates. Maybe another kid had done it and it was copycat stuff, I can't remember. I'd clearly had enough. I turned left and went up Richmond Drive into Vine Walk, a wooded area, and kept walking. On the path a woman walking a dog approached from the other direction. She didn't ask me why I wasn't in school, which was what I expected.

'Hello,' she said. She sounded very posh.

'Hello,' I answered and tried to continue past.

'Do you know what kind of dog this is?' she asked.

I stopped and looked at it. It returned my gaze and panted as dogs do.

'Err...no,' I answered. Where's this going, I asked myself.

'It's a reeeeeeed...'

I thought I'd better join in. 'Reeeeeeeeeed...' I didn't have the answer; I was just playing along.

'A reeeeeeeeeed setter!' she said. We both laughed for moment, I said it was a very nice dog, she said goodbye and off she went.

I carried on for while then looked back. She'd gone. I then darted to my left, off the path into the ferns and undergrowth and lay down on my back, looking up at the blue sky, which was framed by a circle of ferns and the trees. I was stock still; birds sang, insects buzzed, dogs barked in the distance. The scent from the white spring flowers was almost overpowering. I was fixed on the clouds drifting by. Five or ten minutes seemed like a lifetime. What now? I was out of ideas. I must have thought better of it and returned to school; the lady with the reeeeeeed setter had unnerved me. She was a kind, eccentric lady who'd bumped into young boy alone in a wood. It could have all been very different. I now shudder to think.

The next thing I remember is being pulled out of class and taken to the headmistress's office to see the deputy head, Mrs Leighman. Not an unpleasant lady but she was always impressed by kids' dads who were policemen, for some reason. Maybe she was a transvestite freemason or something. I walked in with my eyes down; they met a pair of long legs in denim. I followed them up. They belonged to my Uncle

Brian.

Uh-oh!

He was seated, arms folded, a face like thunder with gas-flame eyes.

Mrs Leighman explained that the other kids had said that I might be at the boating lake, so they'd made enquiries.

Over to Brian: 'Andrew, why did you do this?'

I began to mumble a half-baked explanation. 'You did it because you're weak. WEAK!'

It made both me and Mrs Leighman jump.

He sat back and sighed. There was a pause and he leant forward.

'Andrew, I've never raised a hand to you, but I guarantee, if you pull a stunt like this ever again, you'll go over my knee.'

He tied things up and apologised to Mrs Leighman. He said we'd talk again later. I dreaded a rehash at home that night, but he must have been distracted by something as he didn't show up, but I got the message. He was right. You can't run away from your problems. Just like him, they'll be sat there waiting for you when you stop running. I tried to never do that again, although on occasions through life I might have failed.

The positive outcome, and there most often is one, was that from then on, Mrs Leighman and her colleagues might have been a little less dismissive of Mum and me at parent's evenings. They'd judged a book by its cover and written us off. They hadn't counted on the love, care and concern that was hidden within.

Years later, I clashed with Dwayne when we were thirteen or so, at secondary school. Maybe he'd been bottling all that up since that night at the school gates. Hand-soaped Sid Vicious spikes had replaced the

Spock look by then, also replicated by his younger brothers like mini hedgehogs !

I was told by some shit-stirrer that Dwayne been bad-mouthing me using those 'names.'

I confronted him at the end of a French class as everyone made their way out to the next lesson. He confirmed it, bold as brass. What the hell did he expect would happen next? Did he think I'd moon-walk out the classroom, chanting Hare Krishna? If so, he'd be 20 years too early for that malarkey. My response was physical. There was no filter, no restraint, just instinct.

He staggered back against the teacher's desk, the momentum rolling him onto the top with his feet in the air, as if in John Wayne bar fight. When the kinetic energy from the impact had dispersed, he came off the desk sideways and dropped unsteadily on to his feet. His eyes were full of indignation. He took a second and drew a deep breath with his palm against his jaw then let fly with the full verbal tirade, working through the list. I let him finish and stepped forward. Dwayne moved back against desk cowering, awaiting the inevitable follow up of a total onslaught. At least one punch and kick for each of those 'names' he'd just screamed in my face at the top of his voice. Except it didn't come. What would it prove? What lesson would it teach him? Just to think those things and not say them? He was way below my league physically. Those words were the only attack he had, and they didn't actually hurt emotionally anymore, I was a bit embarrassed because everyone had heard them, including my cousin Andrea who was in the year below and waiting outside for the next lesson.

Whatever it took to steam into Dwayne in that moment, I was thankful that I didn't have it any longer. It was gone. I was learning.

Dear Violence,

We've had a good couple of years, and we were always going to get together sooner or later. At one point I couldn't have made it through without your help. Together we'd settle scores and set my world right. The names stopped and all that shit. I got respect. But now it's not the same, I found The Way and things are different now. It doesn't feel right anymore. Just using each other in the moment. So, let's call it and part as friends.

But I'm sure we'll meet again, some sunny day...
From Andy, aged 13 years.

Finally, the supply teacher intervened, and we were marched to the office of her husband, Mr Bewes. 'We seem to have a racial dispute,' she said in her plummy accent.

Mr Bewes saw himself as a bit an alpha in amongst the ranks of tweed, staff room smokers. A bit of a hard man. One of the select pair that are chosen by the headmaster to attend canings with the task of holding you down on the desk when you won't bend over, one on each arm, while the headmaster gets stuck in. This was a sink secondary modern not a public or boarding school so thankfully they only got stuck in with swings of a cane and nothing else.

There Mr Bewes sat, all sweaty and sanctimonious as we stood before him.

'I've got ginger hair and that's the same,' he said.

His wife wafted away, her pheromones and musk perfume doing little to offset the TRIBO (Teachers Regulation Issue Body Odour) emanating from her hubby.

This could go either way, I thought. Which outcome would go down well with his wife? After all, she'd marched us in there. Did she want to hear from the merciful warrior that evening over dinner or the iron straightener? We were both injured parties, Dwayne and me. He'd already taken a dig and was a gibbering wreck and I'd had Oswald Mosley's Greatest Hits screamed in my face. Will Bewesy try and whack us both, solo, with no back-up? It was a tall order that could get messy, even for this he-man. He'd got to thrash us both or neither.

'I can't go around hitting people just because they call me gingernut, can I? No!' he blurted and leaned forward slapping his hands on the desk. Was that supposed to make us jump?

'So that's it. That's life, it's just the way things are. Get used to it.'

Was he trying to tell us that beneath the macho exterior, there was a little soul that had weathered the lifelong scourge of gingerists? They'd mocked his carrot frizz at every turn, and he'd just turned his ruddy cheek? He'd never ever lost it and lashed out at his tormentors?

Dwayne and I looked at each other quizzically, then back at him.

'OK. Shake hands and go away,' he said.

'No chance, sun dance,' we said in unison. Not verbally of course but loud and clear with our body language.

'OK then…. just GO!'

Merciful warrior it was then.

'Yes, you ginger cunt!' I shouted (in my head).

From then on, there were no more incidents between Dwayne and me. We got along and exchanged pleasantries in passing, even in adult life. He started a family shortly after leaving school and worked for his in-laws. I had eye contact on occasion with his mother over the years too. She knew that what had happened years before at home time shouldn't have, or at least the way it did. I could see she was on the level; there was regret and respect; no words needed to be said.

A very nasty seed had been planted in Dwayne's head by someone and it had led him into bother. What is said and done indoors in the early years can take a lifetime to come to terms with. My disadvantages were plainly obvious, those of Dwayne and his ilk are less so - Ma and Pa plus 2.4 kids etc. Nobody notices if the wounds aren't visible.

As Roxy Music identified: 'In every dream home; a heart ache.'

Better dadless, alone and on the receiving end that night, years before, than a walk in Dwayne's shoes.

Back in junior school, Dwayne had been taken to Karate lessons by his dad along with another of my class mates, Jim, and he'd passed gradings all the way to brown belt two gold tags, the one before the coveted black belt.

At the time, I'd bullshitted him that I had the same grade and was giving it a rest but would be starting back soon: a pathological fantasist lie, from an insecure child. Harsh, but that's what it was. I'd have loved to have been taken to Karate at that age but there was no way for me as Mum didn't drive and we couldn't afford it anyway. There was a judo club at the traffic lights, but it didn't catch my imagination.

With Karate, boxing etc, it's one thing for a child to want to do combat sports because they're interested and another when your dad is marching you in there because he wants you to be hard and not scared of bigger boys like he still is.

Years later when, at the age of 23, I achieved Karate 1st dan black belt for real, under my own steam, graded by the late great Barry Nash, it meant

47

so much to me, remembering the childish lies I peddled to Dwayne and Jim as a kid and, in some strange way, I owed part of it to them.

6

FROM VIOLENCE WITH LOVE

The hexagonal living room was the heart of our house. A gas fire was on the furthest wall with the star-shaped clock above. Like most UK 1970s interiors, the décor was the chintz-tastic antithesis of IKEA/Habitat cool. We had a purple and green swirl carpet, a flower-patterned sofa and two black PVC swivel chairs.

In early years, I'd fit in beside Mum as she sat in hers, next to the standard lamp. Anything scary on our TV (usually a rubber monster on Dr Who), which stood on legs opposite in the corner, and I'd shrink down and bury my face between Mum's arm and the back of the chair. The cliché of hiding behind the sofa was too risky. It would mean breaking cover between the chair and the sofa, exposing myself to whatever danger was on screen. No, Mum's arm and the chair was a much safer bet. It was bad enough running the gauntlet of reaching the gate before the Wagstaffs got to me on the Green.

Since I'd encountered the other side of life out on the Green and come home crying, the advice had been the same from everyone at home: stick up for yourself or hit them back. For a long time, I had no answer.

Mum had explained that she couldn't wrap me in cotton wool, she couldn't always be there. I liked the idea of sticking up for myself but there were barriers to following the advice. Abject fear, a lack of aggression and an absence of physical strength - my food fad had seen to that.

There are grown men out there who genuinely have never had a real physical fight. In the past, I've been guilty, in my shameful ignorance, of snorting with indignation about these people, so twisted was I by the macho currency of violence which I experienced. Were they serial avoiders and cowards with no bottle? Not necessarily any of those things.

Maybe they'd just never been in the environment, back to the wall, where they had to hit someone, even in retaliation. Or perhaps they hadn't been pushed to that point of explosion over time. What I call the David Banner moment, where control is lost, and rage takes over. Were it not for my exposure, I believe that I would have been one of these men, as I don't have a natural inclination to physical aggression. It was brought out of me by those who did have it, Straw Dogs[7] style, and for a while I couldn't get the genie back in the bottle.

As the anger grew from deep down, year on year, the black swivel chairs in the living room would play their part in preparation for that moment. I'd begun to use them as a punching pad to take out my aggression. Teaching myself to form a proper fist, curled up tight, thumb over the first two fingers, and hitting something hard. The PVC-covered chairs had

---

[7] Straw Dogs - controversial 1971 movie. Plot: a gentle academic returns with his new wife to a remote part of Cornwall where she grew up. He is bated and ridiculed by the local thugs. Things escalate, his wife is assaulted, and the academic has no option but to finally respond to his tormentors in kind.

the right amount of give and recovered from the indentations of my little knuckles without a trace. So, I'd privately rehearse, laying into the chair with my right hand and holding it with the left. How long I practised I don't recall. Around nine years old, I was growing in confidence and anger; by now I'd had four years of it.

Stewie Snark was a year or so older than me and a frenemy. On some days a pal, on others a tormentor. His parents ran the Mace corner shop on the corner of Briar Way. One day, he had his nasty head on and bated me right outside my gate, so I had a go.

I was totally ineffectual; he struck back. Bang! My upper lip sandwiched between his fist and my teeth. I burst into tears. He burst out laughing. I ran indoors with my lip growing like a life raft to twice the size. My Auntie Margaret was visiting. We went straight down to the corner shop and she gave it verbally to Mr Snark, who was serving customers.

'He's given him a thick lip, look at him,' Margaret yelled and pointed. 'Our Andrew's two years younger and smaller than your lad! Tell him to pick on someone his own age or I'll be back.'

Mr Snark shrank behind the counter.

I'd had similar problems with a Sheffield family, the Gisburns, on Sandbeck Avenue. It was the name-calling this time, and there were three of them, all big and fat. While Margaret gave it to their mother on the doorstep, they were at the window taking the piss. All, like Bingo, are reformed characters in adult life, one of them a local councillor, I might add.

More work was needed on the swivelling chair. The practice had not crossed over to successful execution. Thumping the chair was one thing, but it didn't hit back like a real live bully.

Next was Munter and Pugson of the back roads.

I fancied my chances now with Roy Pugson, but he was being slippery. I'd been saying I was going to get him. He was keeping away. One day though, I saw the pair of them, again, right outside my house. Pugson spotted my reticence. I was outnumbered. He pointed at Gary Munter.

'You want him, don't you?' he said.

Now was the time. I tried to grab Munter, but he was much stronger. Wiry like a Jack Russell terrier, he pinned my arms. I was spread-eagled against the hedge. His nose was up to mine. I couldn't move. He smelt like biscuits.

'Just because your aunty's in there,' he snarled and nodded over my shoulder to the house. 'You can't beat me.'

He was right. If he'd thought of it, he would have nutted me. Thankfully, he didn't as I was wide open and totally defenceless. It would have been hard to live with after the dig from Stewie Snark. Munter let go and backed away. The pair of them sloped off, like hyenas, to their own territory on the back road. I'd failed again but was physically unscathed this time. My intention to fight back was there and I was going in the right direction. I was starting to stick up for myself but it wasn't my Auntie that Munter had to worry about, but another avenger, four months older than me and a third taller with Milky Bar Kid hair.

Math's school, Seathorne, was at the other end of town and three miles from where he lived, just off Drummond Road. They had different holidays to us. He knew full well who my tormentors were, and they were mysteriously absent whenever he was at our house. I could play outside without any interference.

I was in the school yard one morning at play time and I heard my name shouted. There was a hole in the hedge at the end of the back road. Math was there sat on his racing bike. He'd said he was coming but I'd thought no more about it. He stood his bike against the hedge and dashed into the playground. The blond flash was making a beeline for Mr Munter; it was as if the other kids and the staff members watching over us didn't exist. He reached his target, gave him the message and was out through the hedge and tearing off on his bike in an instant. I'd seen it. Munter got it, and everyone else was oblivious. Like an under ten-year old's SBS raid.

It felt good to be defended and protected. I knew full well by then what it meant to be dadless, but aside from that void, there was a special, spontaneous love demonstrated by different elements of my family, unplanned and uncoordinated. This wasn't The Godfather part 2, more like Bugsy Malone. We were just kids and Math wasn't any competition for Gypsy Rose Lee on the Amusement Park, but he told this bully his fortune free of charge. It meant the world to me. I didn't hear from Mr Munter again.

Dear Andrew,
It's been on the cards for some time that we'd get together and I know you had a couple of tries without me.
But now I'm here for you. You're ready. Things have been building up inside you and coming to a head, you've had years of it and you just can't take it anymore. Well, we're gonna set it all straight between us.
Telling the teachers and dinner ladies hasn't helped. Math's done his bit and I'm working with him too, but he can't be there all the time.
But now the name calling, and all the rest will stop because we're going to stop it. Together. From this day forth.
From Violence

They weren't all wrong 'uns off the back road.
Right behind my house a new family moved in. A boy
my age with a terrier dog called Scooby, plus an older
and younger sister. Pete Davies: he was a real live wire
and for a couple years we had a lot of fun.

His distinguishing feature was his copper red hair,
inherited from his dad. He was a little shorter than me,
but Pete had physical confidence; he boxed
competitively and introduced me to football. We'd
play every day on the far side of the Green, as if there
was one thing that gave Mr Moyer next to us a David
Banner moment, it was a football going in his front
yard. It wasn't a pretty sight and I wasn't exempt from
his ire, so the other side of the Green it was. I didn't
want him reaching for the crossbow!

It was May 1979, the first FA cup that I was
aware of, and it was a great event. Pete was a
Manchester United supporter and even had the kit. I
was rooting for Arsenal as, when we were in town, I'd
bought a little magic picture of Alan Ball that changed
to kick when you flipped it back and forth. I liked the
white sleeves with red shirt too.

We played out in the morning before the game. I
was all eleven Arsenal players and Pete was all Man
United. When the time came for the kick-off, we went
to our homes to watch and agreed to meet after it was
done. Arsenal did it in extra time with a last-gasp goal
from Alan Sunderland.

I was on the Green first then out came Peter. His
team had lost, but he was smiling; he reached out and
shook my hand. This was another first, a proper
handshake. This Pete knows all the man stuff, I
thought.

A year or so later, I'd join Pete's boxing club too.

Math had been going for some time at the old location at the Pier. It was now based off Wainfleet Road, up a slippery wooden stairway. It was run by the Barker family at that point, who were Scottish boxers. The youngest, Gavin, was brilliant, but Pete was his nemesis and could hold his own with him in the ring.

The boxing club was a real spit and sawdust affair, no frills. Stale sweat and leather. We could all see our breath when we walked in; it was ice cold until the training started. There were a range of punch bags and balls, a small ring, rusting mirrors and weights. There's a baptism you receive when you've been attending for a while and spar for the first time; the inevitable smack on the nose followed by streaming eyes. It must numb the nerves, because the next time that doesn't happen.

The rum lads were pooled there from all the schools in the area and enduring friendships were formed. Apart from us little ones, there were big lads like Gary Marsden, Andy Bettany and Steve Stringer, who were probably 16 or so. When they hit the heavy bag, the room shook. There was no real bullying; everyone was friendly. It wasn't too rigid or tough, but it did have its own code and rituals. When you sparred the likes of Gavin, it was best to just cover up because you couldn't lay a glove on them. Nobody hurt anybody though; the coaches made sure everything was controlled. A proper boxing club, as stated above, is not a place for bullies. There's always someone tougher across the room and if you stick it in to others, you'll soon be introduced to them. That was made clear to one and all.

Occasionally they'd take us for a long run (about a mile!), introducing us all to a stitch, the pain in the side you get from expanding your diaphragm with heavy breathing; an equivalent to the streaming eyes from the nose punch, it soon went off and didn't come back again.

There was an annual night of boxing organised through the ABAs[8] where boys from the area would compete. Alf, the trainer, was looking for takers. No way, Jose! Messing about at the club was good for me but to actually step in the ring, no chance. I'd graduated from the swivelling chair, but I wasn't at that level. Pete and Gavin were though. I didn't go to watch on the night either, probably in case I got pushed in the ring, but Math did and reported that Pete had stopped his opponent very quickly, leaving his nose like a flat tomato.

I picked up more soft social skills as a Sea Cub. Brian had taken me one afternoon, a year or so earlier, out into the Wolds, where the Sea Scouts, the older boys, were camping. He stuck me straight into the middle of them. They were cooking and shared their inedible chips with me. After that, they found a tree over a river. Someone climbed up and tied a rope and they all took turns to swing across, everyone splitting their pants in the attempt, which was a laugh. So, it was the Sea Cubs, the miniature version, for me afterwards. A couple of kids from the Richmond went but most were from other schools. It was run by Mrs Watkins and Skip Broughton, and we had kids from the local children's home too, a fate from which I'd been saved by my mother's family.

One boy from the children's home, Mark Castillo, had Special Needs. Someone said his mum used to hit him on his head with a frying pan and that was why he was like that. He was nicknamed Elvis and we all looked after him and each other. It wasn't sentimentalism; they were instilling kindness in us,

---

[8] The Amateur Boxing Association

along with other important values.

One year, at the last cub meeting before Christmas, we played games and got small presents, which wasn't unexpected. Skip Broughton said before we left that we should enjoy ourselves but always remember those less fortunate on Christmas Day too. It took him seconds to say, but I never forgot it or him because of that and, when that time of year arrives, it always comes back to me.

We would all be going to new schools after the summer. From our estate, Pete and Andy Gowling had passed the 11+ and would be going to the Grammar (ultimate intended destination: university, white collar professions). They'd passed under their own steam, not by being coached by 'Mrs Whatchamacallit's hot-house out at Anderby. The rest of us would go to the Lumley or Morris, taking the stigma baton from our parents (ultimate intended destination: blue collar manual labour, the trades, the forces).

At last, Math and I would be there together at the same school. We were very excited and also aware that there would be a coming together with kids from the County Junior, so we put the word out that certain top dogs, sorry, pups, would be on our mind. Over the summer holiday, I'd linked up with some kids from the other side, namely Turtle and Rob. I had a season ticket for the swimming pool and went every day except Sunday, when I helped at the boating lake. We didn't see the main offender until we went back to school because he couldn't swim.

I'd grown in confidence and in an altercation with an older boy at the pool I'd steamed in with fists to the amazement of Turtle. To my shame, on the next sighting of the boy I got stuck in again, without warning. That's the problem. The victim strikes back and can walk tall, but you get a taste for this new flavour, the smack and thump of your knuckles on a face. The feeling of supremacy and dominance. Awful. We all know power corrupts the best of us. Due to the long suffrage, the victim can easily cross the line once confidence grows and find him/herself is now the bully.

I thought I was setting the scene for the new school and the warnings that had been issued. Unfortunately, Math and I weren't in the same tutor group or House at first. I was in with Barney, the only other black kid in the school, maybe down to racial profiling. He was a year older and no body whose chin was in swinging range of his fists bothered him, only the occasional smart arse 5th years but he'd retaliate verbally, and they'd walk off laughing.

We new 1st year boys all met in the yard in our new oversized uniforms on the first day. There was no reckoning, we all came together. There was no need to fight in our own year. We were part of an unusual baby boom, a group of twenty wayward boys, instead of one or two.

(A few years later in the casual era, it would be known as the Jade Gang. Everything is relative but there weren't the same horrors associated with gangs that there are today, knives, guns, drugs and the rest, but there was the spectre of football hooliganism. If Math was the gang's Top Boy, then Simon Pitcher was its spiritual leader and the church, for them not me, was that of the Leeds United Service Crew.)

I was reunited with Zara, whose imprint had remained despite constant other romantic interests. We were in puberty with all that entails, but my fascination still wasn't carnal - just the same heavy crush. She made my heart leap on sight. Our contact was restricted to hand-holding, walking her home from school every day and a very rare kiss, generally encouraged by her sister and Wendy Moakes. I bought and received my first Valentine, and against a soundtrack of the likes of Visage and Ultravox on the TV and radio, and 45s such as James Coit's Black Power and Cal Tjader's Soul Sauce on my little turntable at home, each day was exciting. Life was great. But my long-term adoration of Zara had an unpleasant side-effect, combined with fluctuating hormones: mood swings and jealousy.

I found myself sat next to a boy called Roger. He was unusual because he was from a place called Burgh that I'd never heard of. We hit it off instantly; he was full of beans, laughed a lot and we shared the same sense of humour.

His home life was unusual too. He had a brother a year younger and he wasn't dadless, but his dad wasn't around. He wasn't on the free dinners list like me though. His mum owned and ran her own business; she was a strong, independent young woman and strict with her boys. They all lived in a lovely modern flat above the shop. He had regular contact with his dad though and spoke about him often.

Of the others in our group, the twins and I had parity in relation to being dadless. They were the youngest of four, with a legendary older brother who'd left the school the year before we'd arrived. Out of all of us, they were the most cocksure, fearless and full of confidence. The 5th formers at the new school all knew the twins, due to their brother, and laughed off their cheekiness. They seemed like men to me; they were massive and had moustaches and stuff.

The twins and I were also put through the ritual weekly humiliation of going out from assembly to collect our dinner tokens, little grey discs, for free meals. Paying for your dinner with them was also excruciating; there was no way of hiding it. As soon as I could, I started paying for my own dinner with my boating lake money, going out with the others to Salt's chip shop at dinner break.

Math and I had decided that, despite the welcome unity in our own year, we would meet any challenge head-on with anyone else, up to and including 3rd years. For the first week, we fought every day and rarely came off second best; one word about my colour would get a quick response. I preferred flash point scraps to meet at the gate after school events. There was too much to worry about and I couldn't retain the anger. After a week, no-one bothered us, our little reputations were cemented.

That wasn't enough though. We were fully aware of the status that had been denied to us and our families and granted to others by entry to the Grammar School, so that was the next target. Through Pete and Andy Gowling, we'd heard that a new mate of theirs, a dark-skinned boy called Jem, had been singled out and was being called nigger by a couple of bullies. We went and discussed this with him, and he confirmed it.

'They won't be calling you that for much longer,' I assured him, and we issued warnings, much as we'd done with the County Junior boys. This culminated in break-time sorties onto the Grammar School, fighting them in their own back yard. While I was rolling around on the floor with Jem's tormentor, a hand clamped around the back of my neck, almost reaching my windpipe, and yanked me up and off my feet like a rag doll. Captured!

I was taken prisoner by the Grammar School sports master, a Charge of the Light Brigade type lump with lamb-chop sideburns, and marched inside their building. I didn't get the whack or any other punishment from our lot when I was handed back over. Although he couldn't condone it, our Headmaster probably secretly admired us. No doubt the Head at the Grammar looked down his nose at him also; after all, we were too small to do any real damage, but we'd engaged our detractors.

For Jem, did my intervention do any good? His tag was affectionately abbreviated to Nigs, which he accepted. I wouldn't. I hope that he shook it by the time he reached University.

Nicola, one of my next-door neighbours was a Grammar School girl.

'That boy you were fighting with's got a black eye,' she said. 'His sister is in my year.'

'Yeah?' I said smugly and puffed up, noticing for the first time that her blue peepers weren't that bad either, or the rest, but she was a couple years older, a few inches taller and basically out of my league.

'It's not a very good one though,' she concluded and flounced off indoors, leaving me, quite rightly, de-puffed.

Turtle and co were much more advanced than me in the football world but, since my kick-abouts with Pete, I was very keen. Simon Pitcher had been a pal of mine back in infant school. I'd polished off all the Jaffa Cakes at his seventh birthday party and his mum was beautiful; the original yummy mummy. He was the captain of his old football team. His dad was the manager of the local Lilywhites football club for grown-ups and came to see the practice where the sports teacher, Sorbells, would select the team. The practice was basic stuff, passing, ball juggling and dribbling around cones. We were told that the team selection list would be pinned to the notice board outside the changing rooms the following week.

The day of the list came around. Where am I? I thought. I stepped back, rubbed my eyes and looked again and again. I went away and came back, hoping that it had been an illusion, that I'd missed something or Sorbells had remembered my omission and returned to make the correction, but it wasn't so.

I could fight at last and win; I had self-respect and was the only one with a girlfriend at that point, who was the prettiest girl in our year. This was a huge blow for me; I felt totally emasculated. I could understand the key picks, hands down: Brent, the twins, Turtle, Simon (captain), Jags in goal, Haggis(sub), Paul Bettany, Waitey, and Roger, but out of the remaining places and subs, why wasn't I there? Wop 'ead was even picked. He was dadless too; not due to absence or abandonment though, his had died suddenly the year before. He was half Sicilian and some bright spark had discovered the derogatory term wop and labelled him with it. But Wop 'ead was somewhat better than Italian Bastard, which we heard one of our group had called him back at his old school when he lost his dad. This guy was at the top of our list for that reason and instantly capitulated when we met him in the Lumley yard on the first day. He was the non-swimmer.

Well, Wop 'ead, or Rob, which was his proper name, would literally prove very instrumental in my near future, so his selection for the team in my place could be forgiven!

Following my failure, I felt like I couldn't meet Zara's azure gaze. How could she be with me? I thought. The others will think less of me too. I think less of me. I felt totally diminished, ashamed even.

Dinner tokens and my omission from the football team were blows in a tender time; another would follow shortly after.

I'd plucked up courage to actually go around to Zara's house one Saturday. It took a lot to go up to that door and knock but, trembling with nerves, that's what I did.

It opened. There stood a tall man with curly blond hair. His eyes were as blue as Zara's.

'Yeah?' he said. He wasn't nasty, but not friendly either.

Zara's gran, possibly his mum, peeped round at me from behind him. I could see a strong resemblance to Zara's younger sister, in her. She was smiling.

'Err…is Zara there, please?'

'No,' he said without a blink. 'She's not allowed out. She's been in trouble.'

'Oh...OK. Thanks,' I said, turned and left.

Phew! Was it worth another try at another point, or would she be in trouble again? I guess, back then, in real terms, as a devoted dad, even if Enoch Powell's portrait wasn't on the kitchen wall, a little half-caste kid coming to the door asking to see your eleven-year-old daughter is when all your nightmares come at once. 'Where did it all go wrong?' he possibly asked himself.

I was told by Zara's sister that her gran had said I was lovely though. Had I met her before at a till whilst shopping with Mum in the distant past? I asked myself.

It was a Saturday afternoon, on the doorstep of my birthday, and I was emitting the scent of Brut from the boxing glove soap Zara had given me for Christmas. We were on the bench outside Tonglets on Lumley Road. Something was wrong. Along the lines of: I said it was red, she said it was green, I agreed it was green, now she says it's red. As the years go by, you pick up the signals a bit quicker. This was a new one for me though. I held her hand.

'Don't touch," she snapped and pulled it away. She was side on to me and refusing any contact with those lovely eyes.

'?'

We now had an audience of her younger sister and her pal, one of the North girls. They seemed to know what was going on and found it highly amusing, especially when the penny dropped with me as to what it was really all about.

I was blown out. Dumped. Finished with.

I can't remember how she put it, but basically nothing was happening, and I was jealous and moody. She wanted to be with someone else and that someone was my friend, Roger.

'Wha…!'

My protestations became desperate, to no avail. This was another brick wall and for what would be far from the last time in my life, I'd hit it (or it me) head on.

There was only in or out, a binary situation of absolutes with nothing in between. Favourable, comfy terms like hip and old school were waiting decades in the future. The referee's decision was final: Out!

Out, in the company of my flares, moulded football studs, shoulder strap kit bag, wing collars and purple Chopper bike. Roger, after all, smelt of "now" and had a Grifter, the chunky nemesis pre-BMX that ridiculed the Chopper and anyone who rode one, especially if it was yellow or purple like mine. We belonged in the bin marked "then".

Out! The realisation ricocheted inside me like a pin ball from head to toe. By the time I stood up, everything looked exactly the same, but the world was completely different. A quantum shift. Or was it me? I'd been caught flush by a three-punch combination: dinner tokens, the team omission, and now dumped.

I was down. The sickening kick, for good measure, of demotion to set 4 in maths would soon follow.

No tears, just shock. How could liking someone beautiful cause so much pain, I asked myself, then off I went, home. I jumped up on to the wall outside the labour exchange on Briar Way and walked the length of it as I always did, but in a daze.

When I got home, Hi-de-Hi was on the TV. I sat on our floral sofa, arms folded, chin on chest and watched in silence.

It was never funny anyway and less so now. It was horrible, grotesque even. Everything was broken.

'You're quiet,' Mum said. 'What's up?'

'Nothing,' I replied.

7

HELLO, MR. LEE

Does our musical awakening tie in with the change from childhood to adolescence? Although the first tunes I can really remember, or indeed sung to my mum, were Chirpy Chirpy Cheep Cheep and Chitty Chitty Bang Bang, much to her amusement. I was around the age of ten when sound and rhythm started to get into my bones. From Easter through summer, whenever I was outdoors, beats and melodies from Botton's Amusement Park could be heard drifting on the wind. Intermingled with the rattles and screams from the rollercoaster were the hits of the day, such as Blondie, The Police, and the Grease Soundtrack (if the reader is way too cool for school... guess the rest).

The hormonal changes raised awareness across my senses, heightening them, like the turning of a vampire. I could feel the excitement tingling with every beat. I remember Tubeway Army's Are Friends Electric distinctly on the car radio one morning as my Aunt Gill took my cousins, Math and Laura, and me to school in her Mini Clubman. They were the new electronic sound that years later I'd find out was a pre-set synthesiser. The Age of Aquarius is lodged in my memory as a soundtrack in their house, real or imagined residue from the hippy era in our rainbow family.

It was a long-held paternal tradition that the first-born son was given the name Michael, usually abbreviated to Mick. This had been passed from my grandad to my uncle but had stopped with some controversy when Mick and Gill decided on the name Matthew for their own son. Mum had said that ever since Mick was a kid himself, he was set on it. Michael went to me as a middle name and several of us have it now.

Uncle Mick had a difficult relationship with my grandad, mainly due to the privations endured by the family from his singular outlook on life detailed earlier. On occasion, the reader will have noted my allusions to Dicken's A Christmas Carol. Well, my Uncle Mick was the personification of the Spirit of Christmas Present - minus the holly berries. He was a giant, jovial man-mountain and permanently bearded. In contrast to my grandad, and probably as a reaction to his experiences of going without as a child, he was a workaholic. He'd be out at the crack of dawn, up and down ladders window-cleaning, back home for the school run, then he'd man his other businesses with Gill. At night, he'd be out again selling shellfish around the pubs on the seafront. When we went for a day out, we kids would be in the back of their Cortina Estate with the seats down. It had the unique combination smell of chamois leather, washing-up liquid from the window cleaning, and vinegar and seafood from the pub rounds (maybe not a Tom Ford bagsy). Along with me, Math and Laura, another cousin, Sean, would be there too. He and his much older brother Mark, were dadless in similar circumstances to me, but Sean, who like Laura would have been about five years old then, tragically lost his mum too, so their family extended temporarily from four to six including my weekly stay.

My Uncle Mick and Aunt Gill were always a stylish couple. Years later, they had fashion shops too, the Bird Cage and Studio 24, but during the summers before then, Mick had a very fixed uniform: denims and a white vest; he had the strength and stature to carry it off. The white M&S vests would be his Christmas present from Mum year on year, and there'd always be a laugh when he shook the wrapped present and feigned wonderment at what was inside.

As a young man, Mick, like a lot of locals in their early 20s, succumbed to Skeggy-itus, its main symptom boredom due to a lack of opportunity. After a summer season as a stage manager at the Arcadia Theatre, he ventured down to the bright lights of London and worked in the West End for a couple of years. This opened his mind to characters that he'd be unlikely to meet in mid-60s Skegness. He naturally came across a lot of famous people at the time, some of whom met him again many years later and became customers when they performed in the town. He told us that at one after-show party, the Beatles were present, and a drunk John Lennon, due to Mick being a big man, was trying to persuade him to fight one of their bodyguards. Thankfully, he declined and nothing happened.

'He could be naughty, that Mr Lennon,' Mick told us.

As he worked up and down Lumley Road, he was very well-known and almost universally liked in the town due to his graft and jolly demeanour. He liked a drink, which seems to be in our DNA, but he was a fully committed family man. I was and remain very proud of him. My Wednesday night sleepovers were to give Mum a break and allow her friend to come around. Occasionally, I'd feign sickness for, although

I generally loved Math's company, we both slept in the garage on bunk beds, as Mick and Gill took visitors for B&B from Easter through summer. It was bit nippy and as I was the youngest and smallest, apart from Laura, we weren't allowed to go to bed at the same time as there'd be mischief, so naturally, I had to go first, so I was asleep when Math arrived. In fact, the feigning sickness was on just one occasion, and I remember how badly it went down with Mum. Our mums' sixth sense tells them when we're truly sick and when we aren't, so she no doubt knew but wouldn't force me to go against my will. To her chagrin, she had to call Mick and Gill to explain. I'd buggered up her well-deserved bit of me time. I feel awful to this day about that, although it was just one occasion. I was dadless, yes, but I had a mum who never put herself before me or any of her charges in any way. I can say now that maybe she should have done, but that just wasn't Mum. While I'm at it, if the reader will allow, I'll confess to two other biggies that are etched in my memory.

The first time was when I said goodbye to a particular unnamed phase of childhood innocence, by searching for and discovering wrapped, hidden Christmas presents. I couldn't resist the temptation. It was pure instinct. I plucked the apple and took a bite. The apple in question was the iconic action figure of the Six Million Dollar Man, resplendent in red tracksuit, with condom arm revealing bionic technology. I remember the smell of the fabric and plastic, pleasure and guilt combined rising like an atomic mushroom above Santa-saki. Was I caught in the act? No. Did I confess or try to put everything back in the vain hope that it wouldn't be mentioned, and life would resume as normal? Possibly, I can't remember. Was I in tears and distraught when confronted and fully aware of Mum's disappointment? Yes.

The second was when I smashed the back room chandelier practising nunchakus indoors, like a total mug. Three things you do when learning to twirl nunchakus. Crack your head. Crack your elbow and smash chandeliers. It is said that new dogs destroy houses; add to that, teenagers with nunchakus.

I was only in possession of them because, complicit with my obsession, Mum would have written the cheque or postal order to get the nunchakus from Combat Magazine, which I'd reimburse from my boating lake money. Broken glass for her trouble. Tears from me again. I was way too old to cry by then, so let's keep that between us. OK?

I must have given Mum many other disappointments over the years but they're the ones I specifically remember. I'm sure she'd laugh them off now and I don't ever remember her raising a hand to me, putting me down mentally or blocking any aspiration, not once. Mum knew the score from day one. She saw the hand I'd been dealt and knew what I was up against. But good or bad, the hand must be played, and we played it together over the years of my childhood. (It was only a chandelier. Sorry, Mum)

Math's was the first record player I came into contact with. He had two 7-inch singles: The Boomtown Rats' Rat Trap, which didn't mean much to me and Jaws, you know, the two-note cello signature in the film that tells us that the water will soon turn red. This record meant even less.

Enter Northern Soul. Naturally, the party was all but over by the time Math, then me in his wake, got into it. We were just kids, after all. We certainly wouldn't be going for an all-nighter at Wigan Casino, even if it was still open. Ten o'clock on a Friday night was our limit for Starsky and Hutch. But we did have all the paraphernalia on a pocket-sized scale:

'45 collections, casino classics, beer mat jackets and tank tops smattered with sewn on patches, and bell bottoms with black polyveldt shoes.

We were just mimicking the generation of older brothers and sisters that were 18-21 and doing all the above for real.

On my next birthday, I woke to find a record player resting on my legs. Mum had also got me some records to play from the second-hand section in Woolworths: Jingle Bells by the Greedys (whoever they were) and the Pina Colada song (remember if you're too cool …).

There were several outlets for records back then. Sales of records from that era were stratospheric compared to recent years across various formats.

The shops included the aforementioned Woolworths, Yates and Greenhough on the other side of town and the proper record shop, Herrick Watsons. Herrick's had atmosphere, kudos and vibe. It was palpable to me as a twelve-year-old. They catered mainly to the older mod, punk and skinhead population of the town. Before discovering albums, a couple of years later by way of Tin Drum by Japan, it would be the very occasional '45 for me, post-Northern Soul, but the ritual of entering Herrick Watson's would be the same.

I'd probably picked it up by following others, most likely Math as usual. It went as follows: a mooch around the bins, look at the chart then over to the poster rack, dwelling more on Debbie Harry and the Tennis Girl month by month until I saw it. I'd never seen anything like this: the stance - looking directly, forward feet shoulder-width apart, narrow waste, V-shaped torso. The hands outstretched, holding an object horizontally above eye level. Two black sticks with a connecting chain. I then heard a name I'd first come across back in junior school, accompanied by the fact that he was dead, like someone called Elvis.

It was then spoken by whomever I was with: 'That's Bruce Lee,' they said, 'And they're rice flares.

8

WAY TO THE WAY

The S Saturday teatime diet of David
Carradine's Kung Fu had long been served and
digested, with regular re-runs, ever since it first
aired in the early 70s. As the years passed, the
philosophical exchanges between Young Caine and
Master Po alternated between making more sense or
none at all. On a visit with Mum to our family in West
Yorkshire, I'd bought Vince Morris's Karate-Do[9]
Manual[10] with my boating lake money. On the train
back, I read it voraciously, absorbing its
comprehensive underpinning knowledge of all
aspects of the art. This would be a couple of years
after bumping into Bruce Lee in Herrick Watson's.

I'd then planted the suggestion with Math that we
should start Karate for real. He was game, as was his
pal Kenny, who was the youngest of a large and
prosperous family, owners of arguably the best fish
and chip shop in the town. It was agreed between us,
and Uncle Mick drove us over for our first real-life
Karate lesson. I wore my Lonsdale track suit to take
part, but Math and Kenny were kitted out in brand

---

[9] Do- (pronounced doh) translated as the way, or spiritual path.
Karate-Do: the way of the empty hand
[10] Morris PMV, The Karate-Do Manual (Barrie & Jenkins 1979)

new, fresh white, Karate gis [11] from Palmer's sports shop on High Street.

Palmer's offered a different experience on entry from that of Herrick Watson's record shop, down the road. It was a cramped outlet, where fishing rods and flies would share window and counter space with darts trophies, skating kit, football and boxing stuff that gave the place a rich, leathery scent. It had a long glass counter, where you would be face-to-face with the shopkeeper, who didn't appear 'as if by magic' but was plotted up behind the jump, offering immediate eye contact. There was little wiggle room for hanging around. In seconds, you'd be all mooched out and in need of an answer when asked if you needed help, as 'Just looking,' would be finished by the time you reached the 'g.' My mother was angry when I told her, on one of her visits, that Math and Kenny had their gis from the first lesson.

'If that's good enough for them, it's good enough for you,' she said.

She agreed to get my gi, but on one condition: I had to get a grip on my times tables, as I had ended up virtually innumerate from my time at Richmond Drive junior. I could hide under the radar no more at the Lumley when our classes were split into sets and, as stated, I found myself in the special needs end for maths, but bizarrely the in A stream for all other subjects. There was no Ofsted back then. If crimes against education were covered by the Geneva Convention, there wouldn't be enough room in The Hague for those apathetic shysters in tweed. There they'd be, packed in the dock, like row upon row of nicotine sardines.

---

[11] Gi- (pronounced key) Japanese uniform for practicing Martial Arts, draw-string trousers and double-breasted jacket. Typically, white canvas for Karate, Judo and Aikido.

The teachers weren't all stinkers at the Lumley though; there were some real stars too. I've taken the liberty of retrospectively writing their reports:

A- for Mrs Reid in Art, who'd also taught our Brian and had the quirk of replying with 'Sir' every time you called her Miss.

A- for Mr Holland in RE. He was a Christian but taught us all about Rastafarianism, the Holocaust, and also dangled the carrot of lessons about Zen and the Martial Arts.

B- for Miss Haydon in history. We were restricted to dry subjects like the church farm museum, when we really wanted wars and the space race, but her heart was definitely in the right place.

A+ for Mr Mott. He took those of us who were virtually innumerate and he rebuilt us, almost starting at 1+1. I'll tell you about his claim to fame. Mr Mott was responsible, as he was sports master at the time, for getting a decent mid-field footballer to play in goal. The boy's name was Clemence, Ray Clemence, later of Liverpool, Spurs and England.

There was one other teacher who deserves a mention. He was an English Master, who had us read Shane and To Kill a Mockingbird, amongst other things. In between passages he'd wax lyrical about his take on the underpinning narrative and life in general. At parent's evenings, he even said nice things to Mum about the stories I wrote, which was very kind. Then, one Monday morning in the yard, I noticed most of the girls were crying. In registration we were bluntly told that he'd passed away, having taken his own life.

His name, most apt, was Mr James Love.

Math and, of course, Kenny, jacked Karate in after a couple of sessions. So, as I had no means of getting there, it was just me and Vince's wonderful Manual again for a while. In the first couple of lessons, it became apparent that my adolescent body was in bad shape. Not fat - I didn't eat enough of anything for that. Just unfit, weak and inflexible. Sweat had poured out of me like a fountain in the warm-up and I couldn't even touch my toes. So, without a club to go to, I reverted to the book's section on calisthenics and stretched and stretched. When the Karate sun finally rose again with my new club, the general assumption there was that I was naturally very bendy and supple, but in truth the flexibility came from hard graft alone in those wilderness months.

Also, within that period, a few other things happened. Me and Bruce got properly re-acquainted. I bought the poster from Herrick's and also managed to get into the Tower Cinema's X-rated screening of Enter the Dragon. The cinema was half-full at best, including a contingent of local skinheads, headed up by my future work-mate Mick Appleyard and the rotund Ted Stroud. Years later, as an interlude at rock gigs, Ted would give renditions of John Cooper-Clarke's poem, Kung Fu International, the final line: 'Enter t' Dragon and exit Teddy Stroud,' would elicit a beered-up cheer from a mixed crowd of bikers, goths and casuals.

At home, I dug out an old broomstick from our garden shed, cut it down with a rusty saw and got hold of a toilet chain. These were the ingredients for my prototype rice flares. Whilst at school, my new obsession became apparent and one lad, Mark Revill, said that he knew how to get hold of proper pair.

'No shit? Tell me.'

'My dad's a black belt in Judo and Karate,' said Mark. 'You need to get Combat Magazine. You can order them direct from there.'

The newsagent's face must have been a picture

when Mum ordered my first copy on subscription, along with her regular Woman's Own. She must have seemed like the forerunner of the lethal granny from the Pixar Madagascar movies.

When my first ever copy of Combat arrived, it opened a portal for me into another world. It was mind-blowing, but not in the same way as finding a dirty magazine on the beach. There was no carnality, shame, confusion or body reaction, and it wasn't exactly top shelf, but twelve-year-old boys weren't really the target market.

Enoeda, the Shotokan Karate master, was on the glossy front cover and the odour of sweets and pipe tobacco from the newsagents added to the exoticism of the moment. Master Enoeda had featured in an old TV advert and was also in the Karate-Do Manual alongside the other greats, Asano and Kanazawa, who was my favourite. Sure enough, between the features on the martial arts goings-on in London, Liverpool, Manchester and Birmingham, there were full page advertisements from shops in these cities with names like Oriental World and Battle Orders. The illustrations revealed that rice flares were actually rice flails (an Okinawan agricultural instrument for beating the shells off rice) and their proper Japanese name was nunchaku or nunchaks, as we called them.

From then on, it went like this: I handed over the money, Mum wrote the cheque, I posted the order and a week or so later they landed. It was like Christmas morning when I got home from school and tore off the wrapping, revealing 12" black lacquered nunchakus, with chrome ball-bearing swivels and a sensible chain. Look out, chandeliers!

We would repeat this ritual on a regular basis, like today's Amazon addicts. Over the next few months, I stocked up publications, posters, Kung Fu shoes and other items of clothing.

On one occasion, I ordered a brown mandarin suit from a shop called Samrai Sports. I missed the incorrect spelling, which should have served as an alarm bell. Weeks, then months went by, and my order didn't arrive. When my mother visited, the problem came up in conversation and off she went. She traced the shop by directory enquiries and gave them hell, adding that she had two brothers who would be visiting them for a refund if it didn't come back by return, and that they should be ashamed as I was a twelve-year-old boy, who'd worked hard to pay for the order. A few days later, a cheque arrived with a full refund, but from an entirely different company.

I saw my mother a few times every year all my life. We spoke regularly on the phone, and she did what she could to support me morally in amongst her other commitments. I mastered my times tables and, true to her word, I obtained my first gi, as promised. She'd also gone toe-to-toe over the phone with shady businessmen to make sure her son got his hard-earned money back.

Years later, in the bleak mid-winter of 1991, an international event would bring the fire out of my mother once again. The music of Madchester had put a smile back on the face of Britain. It was a regional culture, burst off the back of Acid House and specifically Manchester's Hacienda club. Shuffle beats and wah-wah guitars had elbowed plastic pop off the air waves, and the Stone Roses and Happy Mondays led the charge. One of the previous decade's survivors, New Order, added to the summer soundtrack with the football anthem, World in Motion. They'd kicked the greedy 80s into touch, along with Maggie the Sacker, who was finally sacked herself, another cause for celebration. In the bigger picture, we'd also seen Nelson Mandela finally walk to freedom, joined by Eastern Europe as the Berlin Wall came down, but something had to spoil the party. Two things to be exact: the cruelty of England losing a penalty shoot-out to Germany and a major international incident in the Persian Gulf.

Gulf War One kicked off the following January and, soon after, the Iraqi regime flouted the Geneva Convention by broadcasting captured allied servicemen on TV: Flight Lieutenant John Peters, a British RAF Tornado pilot, shot down along with his navigator, Flight Lieutenant John Nichol, in the first days of the war. They were taken to the now notorious Abu Ghraib prison for torture and interrogation by Saddam's feared secret police.

The nation viewed the broadcasts helplessly and in shock as, still in his flight suit with its Union Jack patch toward the camera, a beaten, bloodied and disorientated John Peters mumbled his name. As previously mentioned, a couple of years before I was born my mother served in the RAF. She was a patriot, fiercely proud of her unit, so the Iraqi Embassy got the verbal equivalent of Churchill's fire and steel down the phone. The unfortunate innocent on the other end of the line probably hasn't forgotten it. Maybe that was the first tipping point when Saddam decided to turn it in and pull out of Kuwait. An Iron Lady? Iron Mike? Iron this or that? I can't see any worthwhile human virtue comparable with iron. My mother wasn't animalistic, so I won't use the term lioness either. She was as imperfect as you or I, but courage, compassion, bravery, and kindness are some of the virtues my mother possessed. They were her own.

In summer '83, Uncle Mick and Auntie Gill had a stall

80

in the Lion Market and employed my Auntie Margaret and Mum to man it between themselves. It was close to a food outlet that was run by a big bon vivant called Ron. It takes all sorts and thanks to Ron being so forward and loud I got a way back to The Way.

Ron had let Mum, Margaret and anyone else within a square mile, know that his family all did Karate and his daughter Carol had even represented England, but they trained at the other club at Winthorpe. Margaret told Ron that her nephew had started and was very keen but couldn't get to Burgh to carry on, so it was arranged that I should go and see him, after school, to discuss.

Ron and his son-in-law explained to me what was involved and spoke highly of the club, its instructor Paul and the actual style they practised. He was disparaging about the other club where I'd started, saying in as many words that it was just ultra-violent with little underneath the hard culture.

The particular culture that Ron mentioned needs some explanation, if the reader will allow. On the couple of occasions when I could still get to the previous club, I'd seen my old schoolmate, Jim, doubled over in tears by a thump in the midriff from one of the instructors as he passed. This was without warning as the class was moving up the hall, in drill to the instructor's call. Eventually, Jim staggered to his feet and carried on with a nod of approval from the thumper. I thought this was great. I would be ready, I thought, stomach muscles tensed, and show them how tough I am when it's my turn. Thankfully, my turn never came.

Also, when we'd watched the grading (the exam you take to progress to a higher level or darker-coloured belt) a visiting instructor did the same, this time to a grown man, who was a body builder and lifeguard at the local pool. He didn't go down from the cheap shot. These black belt instructors were the kind of men that worked on nightclub doors at weekends and went from thumping defenceless kids who were entrusting their time, energy and money to them, to punching hapless drunks. The three warnings of urban myth weren't on the menu. I wonder if they registered their hands at the local police station as lethal weapons too.

The old club convinced itself that its training and members were a cut above. It was part of an association headed by a noted ex-military hard man from the East Midlands, who ran clubs with the promise of pain and contact fighting. They wore white 'do' gis, used Japanese terminology and had kata in their syllabus, based on the Wado-Ryu[12] style, but the emphasis was on physicality alone and somewhat sadistic in its methods and outlook. Beyond the appropriation of the Wado-Ryu banner and badge (which featured a fist set within the dove of peace), the organisation had little or no connection or affiliation to the Japanese, who at that time still headed up all the UK styles and associations. They had even named their Ryu after the leader but reverted to Wado after attracting ridicule from the martial arts community.

A select few from their organisation had been filmed wearing construction workers' hard hats, literally demolishing a derelict house, with their 'Karate' as a TV stunt. Arms linked, with trainers on, they kicked down brick walls in unison, leaving their gis almost black with debris. They bowed to the rubble when they'd finished! (Compare this spectacle for a moment with the virtues of the dedicated

---

[12] Wado - The Way of Peace, Ryu- School

Victorian craftsmen who built that house 100 years before.) This probably made headline viewing in the comedy section of the national news in Japan. In addition to houses, they also did the same trick with upright pianos. At the time, I saw nothing wrong in this, as I hadn't seen the alternative. It was a case of in the country of the blind, the one-eyed man is king. I was twelve years old with testosterone rising and was a willing subject in that kingdom, as I knew no better.

Many people got permanently damaged by the training methods adopted in 70s and 80s, partly due to a wilful ignorance of the possible long-term effects, even with the best of intentions. The ultimate truth was missing: that *soft* is as integral as *hard*. Balance is required: male/female, night/day and yin/yang. It was a tradition in the Far East for martial arts masters to have a dual role in communities, the second being that of a healer, with equal knowledge of how to mend a body as to break one. Could those men that knocked the house down and smashed the piano rebuild, finish and tune it to the exact specification? Could they even understand the concept?

My later instructor once said that there are men sat in pubs or on building sites that could take us all on together, simply because they're tougher. Fact. But that's all they are. An end in itself. But they don't profess to know anything about the art of Karate-do. They offer nothing to society, only violence. There has to be something more. There should be no confusion between church hall Karate lessons, for people seeking to better themselves, and the entry requirements of an elite military unit.

Enoeda, that great fearsome man and true Karate master who had graced the cover of my first Combat Magazine in December 1982, passed away in 2003 and has the following quote attributed to him: 'The soul of Karate-do is peace and concern for mankind....it is my wish that people who practice Karate-do should keep these things in mind: a gentle heart, modest attitude and peace for all mankind.' No sadism there.

To finish his monologue, Ron explained that there'd be none of the perversions I've mentioned above, but it was still Karate and very demanding. 'But look,' Ron said, 'with Shukokai[13] you don't have to be built like a brick shit-house to do it.' Intriguing.

I was given the start time, directions to the club and instructions to explain to Paul, the instructor, where I'd been training, and that Carol's dad had sent me.

I arrived on my racing bike at Winthorpe Church Hall, a wooden, shack-like construction set back in a field at the end of Church Lane, on a warm May evening. The attendees and atmosphere were totally different to what I had seen before. The members weren't maniacs at the other club, despite the culture, but the people here were warm and friendly, though much fewer. I did as advised by Ron and explained a little about my background to Paul. On hearing my name, he was impressed that I was Mick O'Connor's nephew. I found out many years later that Mick had been given his first break in his business when Paul had handed him, at no charge, the Ship Hotel contract on Roman Bank, probably worth the same each month as a whole housing estate. I was certainly impressed with Paul, the sensei, his club and this style: Shukokai. The gis the members wore were different, narrower in the leg, and the jackets all had black

---

[13] Shukokai - The Way of People Training Together. Full name- *Tani-ha Shito Ryu Karate-Do Kempo Shukokai*. It is typical, historically, for Masters to name their style after their club/dojo, Master Tani's dojo was called *Shukokai*.

piping around the collar. Very smart, very different. They all had black and gold badges with a kanji[14]-ised fist. The iconic emblem or logo of Shukokai. Their stance was natural and dynamic, with the lead arm outstretched with hand open and the other drawn back in a fist, palm up, resting on the belt. I even loved the name, Shukokai. I remembered it from my bible, Vince Morris' Karate-do Manual, which emphasised that it was a style suited to competition due to upright stance and speed of technique. This was fate. I was hooked.

Paul was not hooked on me though, with my black gi (ever the individual) adoration of Bruce Lee and nunchakus. I soon got the message and integrated with a new white gi from Palmer's to add to the collection. I grew away from Mr Lee (for the time being) and the nunchakus went the way of Star Wars, flared trousers and my Chopper bike.

Paul's brother John was one of the highest graded attendees, with a brown belt 2 Black tags. Like the instructor, the club and the style, John was also different gravy. With his long hair, goatee beard and laser blue-eyed stare he was a cross between Buffalo Bill Cody and Robert Powell's definitive Jesus of Nazareth, with a dash of mad Viking thrown in for good measure. He once stared me out shortly after I started and a few years later had me by the throat as I'd caught him by accident in one of our drills.

'You break my face. I'll break yours,' he growled in his distinctive Sheffield accent, before we were separated. Mum had told me in the midst of my obsessive training, 'No 14-year-old boy is a match for a man in his 30s, so don't put it to the test.' John and I made up and his younger brother Marc, who was

---

[14] Kanji - Japanese classical calligraphy

about 25 then, said, 'Don't worry about it, Andy, he even does it to me!'

He didn't. I found out later that Marc was very highly respected and untouchable. One night when he was out with his girlfriend, three merry off-duty marines had mis-read his slight appearance and his aping of Japan's David Sylvian (Warhol hair and make-up) for vulnerability. They'd started picking on the couple, first verbally then, emboldened by Marc's perceived pacifism, they laid hands on. A big mistake. They found out about this soft man the hard way. Two of them ended up spark out on the pavement; the other one ran off into the night with Marc's kiai[15] ringing in his ears.

John's volatility was part of who he was, and, in some ways, it broke the ice as I was always very wary of him. At Karate, he also practiced the Okinawan Sai, the suite of agricultural weapons which was part of Shukokai's training syllabus and included my old favourites, the nunchaku. He arrived sometimes on a trail motor bike but most often in a small yellow van with his name on the side in copper plate writing:

J.A. Cooper
Painter and Decorator

9

THE LAKE

A short while before my uncle took the boating lake on, three of us, me, Math and Mitch (who was four years older than us), were spending an afternoon mooching around the sea front. In the summer season there was a lot to look at, see and do across the range of locations, even if you had no money. Our days were filled when we were old enough to be out on our own but below working age, under 13 years to be exact.

Please, reader, do not panic, this was not a return to the Victorian era, we were never sent up chimneys! In Skegness, from 13 years of age, most kids took legitimate jobs in the seasonal businesses such as chip shops, restaurants or working on the donkeys (herding the donkeys from their field by road to the beach where kids could be lifted into the saddle and be taken down to the sea and back as a group- lead by a donkey boy/girl) from Easter and Bank Holidays, through weekends until the summer season, when the schools broke up and you could work five days a week. I was three or four years shy of legitimate work age when Brian took the lake on. It was a total game-changer.

But back to us three amigos. We'd been out all day on our skateboards. Math had recently come back from a holiday in the States and had a quality model.

It was even better than the one in the Sportique window, (the other, more upmarket, sports shop on Roman Bank - direct competition for Palmer's on High Street) which nobody could ever afford (it remained in the window when the fashion waned all the way to the 90s).

Mitchell's skateboard was also of decent quality, probably American too. He let me have a go on it once. One push and you seemed to go on forever, a whole different world. My skateboard, on the other hand, came out of the Janet Frazer catalogue that Mum ran as a little side-line, with a few customers on the Green. It was the equivalent of the Stone Age roller skates that were still in circulation in the mid 70s, with the red leather laces and hard black wheels. It was debatable what gave you more mobility, those wheels or no wheels. It even had a name emblazoned in red underneath; it was the Deluxe, and had a rubber brake at the back, maybe in case you had a long run down a very smooth, very steep hill.

It was bloody murder pushing along on the Deluxe, trying to keep up with those two. We'd been to the usual haunts, where there were smooth bits of concrete and slopes to skate on. The Compass gardens, next to the Clock Tower was the number one destination. Another one was a little slope with marigold flower beds either side that led to the boating lake. When we got to the bottom, which would have taken all of three seconds, something grabbed our attention and we collectively picked up our boards and took a closer look. Our eyes were fixed on an abandoned red canoe, which was bobbing at the water's edge in a spoon-shaped inlet. We discussed what to do between ourselves. The canoe was smiling at us and out of view of the main jetty, so we decided in our infinite wisdom, after looking both ways, to board her as the paddles were inside. We'd take our skateboards with us. Altogether, one foot in the canoe.

'Whooooaaaargh!'

Splash!

We didn't understand that boats on water aren't stationary and didn't require a push like skateboards. With the weight transfer, it shot away from the edge and we were all in the drink.

Phase 1: After an initial splashy panic, the first revelation hits you like it hits all those that are baptised in Skegness boating lake for the first time: it's 2.5 feet deep.

Phase 2: You stand up and laugh hysterically, hands on knees for two minutes.

Phase 3: Anyone who's seen and heard this, usually pensioners on the benches, then laugh hysterically for five minutes at your expense.

Phase 4: Next revelation. You try to get out and can't, as the sloping banks are covered in slime, so you slip down and are under again sending you back to phase 2.

After a short while in the phase loop, we decided, as we were all wet through, that we may as well get in this canoe. All three of us. Then it capsized and sank. Madge and Cyril Bluerinse, watching on the bench, then needed to go home and get changed. We soon started feeling cold so abandoned Crazy Horse the red canoe and staggered onto dry land. We also realised that, despite being partially obscured by the inlet, the boating lake attendant had noticed the commotion and was heading our way.

Boys of a certain age don't give up on their day and go straight home; it doesn't come into the equation even if they're soaking wet; so we had the brain wave of going to the public toilets nearby on the other side of the lake to use the hand dryer on our trainers. Mine were quite funky Stars and Stripes canvas plimsoles.

The hand dryer didn't cut it. By now it was late afternoon, the temperature was dropping, and our teeth started chattering.

'Sh... sh... shall we go home?' one of us said, probably Mitch.

'Y...y... yeah, let's g... go home.' We all shivered in agreement. The Deluxe was even heavier with the water absorption and less responsive, as the moody ball bearings in the Fred Flintstone wheels began to rust. I chugged off down the hill of Sandbeck Avenue, as Mitch and Math glided down Drummond Road, like drowned rats on a cushion of air. Maybe three pushes and they'd be home.

There is a crater in New Mexico that has been identified as the site of the asteroid impact that spelt the end for the dinosaurs' reign, and ultimately their extinction. They were cold-blooded reptiles that could not adapt to the environmental changes in the aftermath. In the port of Aden, Yemen, on its own Gulf, there is another crater that is widely regarded as the place where the British Empire finally met its own demise. My Uncle Brian was posted there, amongst it all in his last attachment, as an army driver/bodyguard with the Royal Argyll and Sutherland Highlanders.

They were a notoriously tough regiment, not an infantry elite in the sense of the Paras or Marines, but one that was heralded as one of the most combat-experienced in the British army. Thus, in 1967, they were sent to bring order and Tribal Law to the Crater area of Aden, under the command of the charismatic Mad Mitch - Lieutenant Colonel Colin Campbell-Mitchell, a direct, no-nonsense character, who was seen as something of a maverick by his superiors in Whitehall.

With this attachment came combat experience for Brian. There were daily engagements with an insurgency growing in confidence as the inevitable withdrawal of the British approached. Whilst driving the unit Padre (military vicar), they'd come under attack and took cover. The Padre had stood by the door, against Brian's advice, and got a bullet wound. Brian had fought his way out and got them both to safety. This led to a mention in dispatches.

The young Corporal had risen quickly but would be time-bound for ten years before his next promotion. Following Aden, garrison life in Germany held no allure, and the next stop looked like Belfast, which was livening up rapidly. His family back home had endured some big changes. His dad had passed away and he had two new nephews and one of them was at home with Mum and Nan.

A new decade, new opportunities, only 21 and a man of the world with all this under his belt. Home he came to freedom, enterprise and us at Tennyson Green.

Poker. A complex card game, success in which requires talent and a specific skill set, including strategic intelligence, psychology, complex calculation, innovation, bottle and stamina. These ingredients might also be found on a checklist titled 'entrepreneur.'

There were two groups of poker players that plotted up in the card schools of Skegness Snooker Hall: the social players and the high rollers. Brian was in the latter. The sessions, which took place in smoky electric light, could run from day into night, on through the early hours to dawn and beyond.

Mum recalled that one night or early morning, Brian came in and woke her up. She opened her eyes to see the air full of pound notes, floating down from the ceiling onto the bed, and a red-eyed Brian standing there grinning from ear to ear. It had been a marathon high stakes session and he had won. Plenty to buy a van, a market stall pitch and enough stock to get started with his wife to be, Heather. He was finished with poker; he was now a businessman.

The year after our baptism with the red canoe, Brian won the tender for the boating lake. This was a big step up from a market stall to a prime site on the foreshore: the hotbed area of seasonal commerce nearest to the beach and sea, the ultimate destination for holiday makers seeking to spend cash on fun and entertainment.

Right next to the lake was the former dolphinarium that had been converted into an open-air skating rink for Speedskates. These were the forerunners of 1990's roller blades. On rotation through the tannoy was the soundtrack from the films Grease and Saturday Night Fever. This was all new and very exciting for me. I was there as a helper with no responsibilities, I could come and go as I wanted, and Mum issued tickets behind the counter as she'd done for decades at the Tower Cinema before I was born.

My tasks were bailing water out of the boats with empty orange containers cut in two and carrying the canoe oars back to the boat shed when it was time to pack up. I didn't deal with the customers at all. The boat lads did all that; they were all in their mid to late-teens. Brian inherited some staff for the first year and hand-picked his own from then on. On one occasion, I left one boat and went to do something else; we were busy, and the boat wasn't ready for the customers.

Brian gave me a bollocking:

'When you start something, finish it!' When Brian told you off, he made sure the information penetrated. I took it onboard and never forgot. In my life he never ever got physical; he didn't need to.

For a couple of summers, I was just helping out as described then, once I was 13, I got my seasonal job alongside the other lads, dealing with the customers, mainly on the canoes bailing out as before and pulling the canoes up the concrete bank. My hands soon became blistered and then calloused by the salt water and nylon ropes.

It was the plum job that everyone wanted, out in the sun. The other lads were mainly a combination of Grammar School pupils and coppers' sons. If you didn't fit that category, you stood no chance. There were some rare exceptions, and one was Lee, who would later introduce me to music and playing in bands. He was a tall blond Adonis, four years older, with a rotating following of female admirers who would line up on the wall facing the jetty like groupies. Maybe they were the referees that landed him the job!

Other kids would come back to school grey from a summer in a chip shop or restaurant. Being mixed race, I was dark anyway and my melanin was fully charged up, so I was brown as a berry. I took Saturday as my day off; it was the quietest day and I went to work at Butlins as a barrow boy, but it was tips only and I didn't have the front back then

to charge the punters or push myself onto the coach, as some of the other lads did, so after a couple of weeks I packed it in and enjoyed the day's rest.

The first couple of summers, I was restricted to the canoes and not allowed to use waders as, due to my limited height, if I lost my footing and the waders filled with water drowning was a real possibility. It was annoying nonetheless.

An unspoken fact was that Brian made it very clear that there would be no favourable treatment because I was his nephew; if there were, it would result in me being shunned by the other boys, who were still a couple of years older than me. As if to make this obvious, he over-compensated the other way: harsh treatment and lots of bollockings. I didn't mind and understood the set-up.

Once I was deemed tall enough to use the waders, I was over on the rowing boats, one of the big lads at last that I'd looked across to from the canoe bank for the first few years.

Brian then pushed me out of my comfort zone and had me working late alone or opening up. Taking cash, issuing tickets and giving change was a big step for me. The first time, I got in a right mess. The customer sensed my fear and confusion querying the change I'd given. I folded and gave him his money back and told him it was on the house. I had to get a grip of my numeracy block or walk away. If Brian knew what had happened, he'd hit the roof and the lake would be over for me. The combinations of cash were limited, as were the permutations of sale, so when it was quiet, I got my head round it and clambered over the block.

The red canoe incident that occurred with us and a limited audience years before was played out like clockwork on a grander scale every Sunday afternoon. The pensioners would be plotted up, ready in the prime crescent seats opposite the canoe bank. At 3pm the pubs would kick out, by 3.30pm the drinkers would reach the lake, 3.40pm they'd bought their tickets, 3.45pm they are placed in the canoes and pushed out onto the water, seconds later they'd capsize and be in the other kind of drink and going through the Four Phases of Baptism I described earlier.

Brian often half-joked that we should have sold tickets to the blue rinse brigade on the facing benches. When we were really busy on Sundays and Bank Holidays, he'd tell us in no uncertain terms, 'Don't put two pissed lads in a double canoe. Got it?'

I'd have a look round and if I couldn't see him lurking and the coast was clear, in the double canoe they'd go and two seconds later over they'd roll. Waders on, we'd drag the canoes up the bank, flip and empty the water out and let them have another go. After giving the audience 30 minutes of free entertainment, they'd stumble out onto dry land.

'Where's nearest laundrette, mate? they'd ask.

I'd give directions: 'There's a hand drier in the bogs over there, the launderette's the other way, over there, behind the Tower Gardens.'

Dadless, but with the benefit of luck and association, I had that wonderful character-forming experience of the lake and, by the end of it, I had a hard-wired work ethic, my own money in my pocket and my self-esteem restored.

The last two seasons had been much quieter due to the miners' strike. Seaside resorts had been caught in the crossfire of the political war of attrition between Thatcher and the miners' union leader, Arthur Scargill. The stakes couldn't be higher for the two opposing ideologies. This was the height of the Cold War. The Soviet Union and USA were watching the theatre of battle with vested interest. Whoever would win this conflict, which was played out on the picket lines, and felt in the empty bellies and kitchen cupboards of the striking miners and their families, would assume nation-changing supremacy. Whoever lost would face total annihilation. Domestic tourism in resorts like Skegness was collateral damage and it wouldn't be quite the same ever again.

I left school in June '85 and, after my final summer on the lake, I had to go and sign on, back and forth between the DHSS and the Labour Exchange. It was soul-destroying. That September, some of my peers would find themselves at the mercy of basic training in the military, some would go to college and a few would wear the coveted green blazer as Grammar School 6th formers. None of that was for me.

I explained to the DHSS clerk that I'd hoped to go to art college but had been rejected. I'd taken it as a given for years that Lincoln Art College was where I was heading; I hadn't entertained the thought of a knock back. What now?

'So, you like painting then?' the clerk asked and gave me a leaflet. I was sent down to Lansdowne Road to start on the YTS (Youth Training Scheme). Over the next two years, my character, rebuilt through work and training, would be challenged on many levels, and severely put to the test, as I stepped unaware, into the harsh adult world of the Construction Industry.

10

WE ARE THE RAGGED

The first day at Lansdowne Road YTS centre was a school reunion of sorts, but on a much smaller scale with only me, Jags, Waitey, Eddie and Swanie. We would now be split into trades on the Government Scheme. £27.50 a week would land in our bank accounts (ker-ching!), £10.00 of which would go to Mum for board. The rest was mine. All mine!

The centre itself was just a couple of portacabins really, with a small outdoor training area, a cement mixer and some rusting scaffold poles and planks. It was owned by Roy; his daughter Kaye had looked after me when I was small, so I could do no wrong in his eyes. He also had Big Jay there as the main instructor and Dave Grey, a large hippyish man with a beard and long hair, mainly on admin. Big Jay's cards were on the table: an old rocker with aviator glasses, quiffed black hair, and a gold tooth. He was on the level and had great rapport with us. Dave was his foil: mellow, witty and well-spoken, with a wicked sense of humour.

The idea was that we'd be there just long enough to do some very basic health and safety training and then be farmed out on placement to work with a real firm. True to the Labour Exchange clerk's words, I was put forward for painting and decorating.

A man who called himself Tone turned up. I didn't know whether it was short for Tony or Tone Deaf. He did a very brief interview and agreed to pick me up at home the following day.

Tone arrived at my house 30 mins late, which he did almost every day following. He drove a Zanmobile, a red Citroen 2CV. It had a roof-rack and his tools and materials were in the back. It struggled to get up the hills of the Wolds when we worked out there, with Tone desperately pulling on the choke and on a roll up at the same time.

He explained that he was from Leicester originally and had worked in a factory in Skegness. The factory had closed with redundancies and the foreman there fancied himself as a bit of a painter and DIY enthusiast, so had advertised for work and, being a good talker with a bit of front, he'd landed a pile of customers. He called up his former colleagues, including Tone, to come and work for him (country of the blind...remember?).

After a short while, Tone felt he should do the same. This was the mid 80s; there was a bit of money sloshing about and likewise, his advert had got respondents, much to the chagrin of his former boss.

Tone was a nice man; he accepted me. He hardly moved his mouth when he talked and had the gained the nickname The Ventriloquist due to this. I think he ran out of work, but I wasn't that happy there. He was always late. The staff at the YTS centre were amused because the complaints about time-keeping and trainees were normally the other way around. So, after a spell back at the centre, I got another interview. This time much more professional with Harold Stepney from Stepney & Son. He had bubble perm hair like Michael Knight from Knight Rider and a droopy porno moustache. There was an embroidered company badge on his clean white overall jacket and his trousers were spotless. He looked like an ice cream man.

Harold explained that I would be trained through progression in the different areas of the trade, and there would be a job for me at the end, if I was good enough. He also explained that he'd taken the business over from his dad, Albert, who still worked but wasn't in charge anymore, or so Harold thought. I'd to be at his house at 08.30 the next day. Nice pitch. No problem.

Mum was pleased when I told her about the new placement. The old man, Albert Stepney, was well known, and it was a proper company.

In reality, the previous placement, Tone, would have been better suited in a John Wayne film or the O.K. Corral. I say again he was a nice man, but he was in no position to train anybody, especially not a school leaver, and he shouldn't really have been allowed to do so.

I arrived at Harold's place on my racing bike and was given a pair of Albert's old bib and brace overalls, a white jacket and some tools. I was with Stepney & Son for almost a year. Above me were Digby and Wilsh, aged 21 and 24 respectively, and of course, old man Albert.

The boys were friendly and warm, especially Wilsh; he'd always be willing to teach me stuff and we had a laugh. They warned me about Albert though. I didn't know what the fuss was about as he seemed nice enough to me. Albert was quite naturally old school in appearance, well-groomed with greying slicked-back hair, athletic for his age; not at all doddery. He smelt of Brylcream and Hamlet cigars. Not an unpleasant combination (bagsy alert for Tom Ford). On meeting him, he'd asked about our Mick, as most adults did on hearing my surname, and was initially accepting and friendly. Gradually, it changed.

It was mid-winter, and we were working on a conversion of flats, above Wrates on Lumley Road. This particular contract was, despite everything, a great experience and due to my time on the lake and Karate training, I wasn't afraid of hard work. Stripping miles of wallpaper, running up and down stairs, mixing artex, measuring, cutting and pasting paper, and working outside, burning off, up scaffold.

Outside ... burning off ... up scaffold.

It had been stated that I wasn't to work above two metres in height unsupervised. Wilsh and I were out the front with butane gas cylinders doing the burn off. This involved passing the gas flame from the blow lamp over the face of the paint until it bubbled, then using a tool called a shave hook to scrape it off while it was soft. Then you move along to the next bit systematically.

I dropped my shave hook and shimmied down the scaffold pole to collect it. *Wrong!*

I got to the last stage of scaffold above the roof and thought, sod this, and jumped down onto the roof. *Wrong!*

Sorted. I found my shave hook, climbed back up and carried on.

Wilsh had hardly noticed this, due to the 'whoosh' of the gas and blow lamp and the ice-cold wind blowing in off the North Sea half a mile away.

We worked our way along the front of the building. At some point, butter fingers, I dropped the shave hook again. I followed the same procedure except when I jumped off the scaffold onto the roof:

CRASH!

In the blink of an eye, I'm falling and everywhere around me glass is falling too at the same rate and the sound is still in my ears as I plummet. I instinctively realise I'm in an alcove, so my arms and feet are against the walls either side by reflex, and I remain upright. Due to this I land feet first with my back against the wall twenty feet below, and crumple into a squat. My hard hat bounces twice across the shop floor.

Silence. But I hear blood rushing through my ears and white noise. Adrenaline. Shock.

I get to my feet, still trying to comprehend what happened in the last couple of seconds. My nose is cut.

I hear shouting. There are two voices above and movement. As I look up:

WHACK! A lump of lead hit my shoulder, dislodged from the hole by my would-be rescuers. First Wilsh peeps down through the hole at me then Carl the builder.

They dreaded what they'd find.

Wilsh thought he'd seen my feet disappear through the glass when he heard the crash, and that I'd gone head-first. A sure-fire fatality, 20 feet down, dead Andy and ketchup all over the place.

For comedic effect, it would have been great to strike a match and light one of Albert's Hamlet cigars with Bach's Air on the G String playing in the background[16]. But in reality, I was dazed, and my ears were still ringing. Carl got a ladder down and out I came. Everyone was greatly relieved. I ironically had the nickname Sky Diver for a while afterwards.

The glass roof below the scaffold had been obscured by all the debris, so it appeared to me to be the same as the tarmac I'd wrongly jumped down to

---

[16] The basis of a TV advert that was aired in the UK, in which the victim of disaster drew solace from his cigar.

earlier. It was safety glass reinforced with wire, so it broke into small pieces. If it had been plate glass, I'd have been cut to ribbons. There were no accident books to complete in the aftermath back then either. The building game, as the construction industry was referred to in the mid-80s, was a lot more Tom & Jerry then than now. Following an incident, you'd be patched up, have a fag or a cuppa, laugh the pain off and get back to work. Because this was a 'spectacular,' I was sent home and walked it, as the Green was less than a mile away. Mum made me a sweet tea on arrival. No mobiles then either, so when Harold heard he was straight round to our house. He'd been cool and off-hand since the day I started but now a smiling, warm Harold was there on our doorstep. Mum, courteous as ever invited him in.

We discussed what had happened and Harold said that he'd decided that from what he'd seen, when the YTS was over, he'd take me on as a full-time employee. I took it at face value as I still had a year and half to go and wasn't thrilled about some emerging issues. Was his change of heart triggered by a fear of litigation?

Contrary to what he had told me at my first interview, following the job on the flats I was largely doing skivvying, washing down, cleaning, fetching and carrying most of the time. I have a claim to fame of having washed the nicotine off Skegness Police Station's ceilings with hot water and Flash detergent, which nearly did as good a job on the skin on my hands as it did to the nicotine on the lids[17]. It was like working in a jungle, as the coppers were sitting around all day, heating on full blast, smoking and dealing with the hotbed of crime that was mid 80s Skegness. Not.

---

[17] Lids – decorators' parlance for ceilings

Naively, I thought my character was being tested and I was up for that, but it had dawned on me that it wasn't anything that noble. It was just exploitation. More YTS boys appeared, three of us in all. Three boys being exploited, not properly trained and charged out to customers at £x.xx an hour. Naughty.

Harold's dad Albert's 'race' digs started too. When I told him I'd gone to a Karate competition in Stoke on Trent he remarked:

'That's real *nig-nog* country.'

I said nothing; I didn't know what to say.

One day it was on the radio that Libya had been bombed by the Americans in response to terrorism, and one of Ghaddafi's infant daughters had died in the air raid. I got:

'One less *wog*. I know it sounds callous but…' He trailed off. Where's this going? I thought. I soon got my answer.

One day we went to Albert's house to collect some equipment. I waited outside. Mrs Stepney Senior came out.

'Where are you from?' she said.

Pleased to meet you too, I thought. 'I'm from here.'

'I don't mean that,' she snapped. 'What country are you from?'

'Here, I was born here,,' I answered.

'Where are your parents from?' Back like a flash.

I didn't answer. Would she be asking me for my papers next?

She then went on about being from Mansfield and 'coloured people.' I was dazed.

We'd got the kit we needed so off we went.

Albert had also taken a pop at my grandad, long gone. I knew Grandad drank and so on, but I didn't need to hear that, and worst from Albert.

What kind of man insults a boy's grandad, to his face, for no reason, 16 years after his death?

What kind of a man is telling you about it now, all these years later? You are entitled to ask.

Before joining Stepney's, Wilsh and Digby had been on the original Youth Opportunities Scheme, the YOP. It was the forerunner of the YTS. They were doing local paint jobs as part of a group which was based at the Town Hall. Their instructor supervisor had been John from Karate; he'd taken the job for a couple of years in the economic downturn. He was on a pedestal to them; they knew a different side to the scary guy that I saw from the Karate club. They told many funny stories about their time working under JC, as they called him, and he was cast in a completely different light.

Bob, one of the senior people from Karate was always there to listen after training. I'd confided in him about old Albert's bollocks at work. He heard me out but diplomatically said that it was still important to respect Albert because he was around before I was. In other words, respect your elders and Albert, despite what he said, was an old man. I took Bob's advice, but I couldn't accept what Albert had said. It was a cheap shot.

In the end, I asked Bob to talk to John, to ask if he would possibly take me on from Stepney's. At first, he was anti, mainly due to the hassle factor, but he said I should call him as he wasn't training regularly then, was busy at work and had a new baby also. I explained to John what had happened and also about what Wilsh and Digby had said, which made him laugh. It was a whole side of him that I couldn't imagine before. He said he'd speak to his wife and the YTS people. John's wife weighed it all up and said that as I'd got experience, the Karate factor and wanted to work, to give me a chance. The YTS confirmed that the only outlay was for insurance cover, so he agreed to take me on.

I now had to face Harold Stepney and break the news.

We were at his house and had gone there at the end of the day to unload the van. I asked to speak to him alone. Just the two of us.

We stood in his garage. When I told him, I was leaving, he scoffed, 'So, you don't want a job?' Typical this, typical that, I could see him thinking.

'I do, but not here,' I said. That fazed him, and he stood back.

'Where then?'

I told him and the reason. He was beside himself.

'Why didn't you tell me?'

'How could I tell you? He's your dad,' I said.

He wanted a week's notice. I wouldn't give him one. I told him I'd be there until the end of the week then we'd be done. He even went around to see Mum. Naturally I'd kept Albert's shit from her. She just told Harold that I wasn't learning anything, and it would be better for me training with John.

The lads told me that Harold had got them together and asked if they'd heard Albert say anything bad or racist to me. They all looked at the floor. That was the answer, if it wasn't a no, it was a yes. To his credit, Harold confronted Albert as an employee, not as his dad, and had it out with him. It took a lot for me to stand up to Harold that day. I had bad dreams about it for a while, but the backing of Bob and John from Karate had made it possible... I was 17.

I didn't find Harold to be a particularly warm or likeable man during my time on that firm, but he was still a gent, to be fair, despite some iffy business practices, and none of those things that came from his dad would ever have passed his own lips. Things were what they were; he'd taken on the business and was expanding and moving forward. He wished me well but moaned about my refusal to give a week's notice. The other boys said Harold improved the conditions and training soon after. My immediate future lay elsewhere. For the first time, I'd seized my destiny and made a big decision. It would not be the last.

Everything was different with John. On the first day, I opened the van door and John welcomed me in. I was hit by the reversed seagull cries, totemic drums and shamanic vocals of The Beatles Tomorrow Never Knows, like a psychedelic call to prayer booming from the speakers. As I said, completely different. The soundtrack to and from work was a cassette with the albums Revolver on one side and the White Album on the other, so the education was musical or cultural as we might say today, as well as learning a trade.

This suited me right down to the ground, along with the Karate connection, which was something that had also been very important to John and his family in the past. He also wanted to know who I was as a 17-year-old, where I was coming from and what I thought in comparison to himself as a youth back in Sheffield in the late 60s.

A good tactic, passed on to me by the YOP boys, was to move the subject to his exploits at the end of tea break, which would lead to the kettle going on again and a considerable extension! John got a considerable preview of most of the key events in this book, thity-odd years ago, when I was still wet behind ears, but he gave me time and space to talk, using some of his to listen.

The main work John undertook was private/domestic interiors for wealthy discerning clients and the quality was very high. The jobs were completely different in approach and execution from the previous placements. The other key events, following soon after the new start, were the passing of my driving test and my money going up to £35.00 a week once I was in the YTS second year (ker-ching, ker-ching!).

Back when I was at Stepney's I'd bought a rotten old red Ford Cortina 2000E from Wilsh's mate for £270.00, way before I'd passed my driving test. It stunk of fags and wouldn't have been out of place on the recent TV series Life on Mars.

The car had sat outside the house rotting for a few months after the battery went dead and she wouldn't start. Once I passed my test, Aunty Margaret's husband Dave came around to get her (the car) going. He was at it all afternoon with me assisting and finally, with the jump leads attached to his own car, she started kicking back to life. It was like raising Frankenstein's monster back from the dead. My Uncle Mick gave me his cosmic alloy wheels. With fat 185 tires fitted and a louvre on the back window, the car bore a bit of a resemblance to the Ford Gran Torino, from Starsky and Hutch. It was proper boy racer material! I thought so any way, but when it rained the foot wells would fill with water and John would wait to see if it would start at the end of each day before driving off!

I had to go technically self-employed when the YTS finished, on the basis that if there was work with John I'd be there, but if not, I'd be on my own fending for myself; that was made clear from the off and I was happy with that. Over the time we worked together, we were sometimes joined by John's dad, Stan. He was the reason why John had come into the trade as a school leaver back in Sheffield, against his dad's protestations. It was finally agreed on one condition: he would be apprenticed to the company, but wouldn't be working under Stan for at least the first three years. That moment might come earlier but the company boss would decide if and when. The time soon passed, and when John became an improver, as agreed, he and Stan worked together as colleagues, not father and son.

By the time I joined John, 20 years later, Stan was retired and only came in now and again. If we were working in the Chapel St Leonard's area, we'd go around to Stan and Nora's (John's mum) for lunch. I'd always be made welcome and sit at the table with all the extended family coming in and out, sister, brothers and grandkids. It felt great to be accepted on this level.

When Stan worked with us, I'd often be left with him, while John went to price jobs. He'd have me in stitches with his dry wit. When he was working on step ladders he'd say, with a wink, 'Don't tell Nora I'm doing this, will you?'

A nudge and a wink came with a lot of what Stan said. When I went self-employed, he had a rare serious word with me. Stan explained that as a subby (sub-contractor):

'… you'll be up against stuff moving from company to company, sometimes your face will fit and sometimes it won't, no matter what you do. If you're good you're a threat to the regulars, and if you're less than great you'll be the worst. Sometimes if you're t' best man for a job, some graining or a nice wallpaper, you won't get it or you'll be laid off in place of someone less able. It's just the way it is and it will happen.'

Stan worked as he talked. 'Every big firm's got passengers, the crap ones, shitehawks that shouldn't be there. They're there because that fits.' He drew his finger around his face. 'They're in wi' t' boss for whatever reason and their shifts are carried by everyone else.'

Stan stopped, nudged his hat back off his brow, stood one foot on the steps, and rested his elbow on his knee. Then he pointed at me with his brush handle.

'Most skibos[18] just want to come in and pull their dirty ovies[19] on. You're different, you want graining[20] and you'll find it. You'll always survive.'

He stood up and faced back to the windowsill he was working on, then glanced back. 'It's the way you hold your mouth.' He smiled and winked. Back to leg-pulling and levity.

It was sage advice, that stood me in good stead. I came across it many times over the years in London. John had often warned me of the harsh realities of what he called big firms in big cities. The realities of our trade, and human nature, had been documented by an Irish man, Robert Noonan, a hundred years earlier. His daughter finally managed to get it published in 1914, three years following his passing. She received £24.00 from the publisher for the privilege.

Soon after, both the officers and men in the trenches of the Somme had abridged copies in their nap sacks. The humour and humanity gave them brief moments of respite from their unimaginable situation. As the century progressed, the book opened a window

---

[18] Skibo - Sheffield slang for an unskilled brush hand. 'Tosher' is the London equivalent.

[19]Ovies - slang for overalls

[20] Graining - an advance decorative craft mimicking hard wood, originating in France introduced to Britain in 1783 by the Crace family.

for the uninitiated to look through into the bitter existence and plight of the working man...Noonan's book has changed the world. He is better known as Robert Tressell [21].

Stan had lived it in Sheffield as a painter with a large young family to feed on his return from the war. When he got back, like so many others, he was a stranger to his five-year-old daughter. In the evenings he'd struggled on the bus with his paste table and tools, doing private jobs to make ends meet. This was after a ten-hour shift on site for his regular employers. Once, exhausted, he'd fallen backwards off a plank while papering a ceiling and damaged his shoulder. He couldn't let on, not even to Nora. He worked on through the pain; he had no choice; he'd have lost his place, Christmas was approaching without relent and he'd make sure it was a good one.

There he was, all those years later, a retired grandad, helping out his son and passing this knowledge on to me, his son's apprentice. Stan enjoyed the company of young people, which included me, and he had no time for grumpy old men like Albert Tatlock from Coronation Street, who banged on about the good old days. He said it a was lie, plain and simple, they weren't good old days, it was bloody terrible.

Stan had always said that when city people like him come to the seaside it seems like toy town, or Noddy Town, as he called it.

'Nowt's to scale here. The stinkos, villains, hard men, and the firms - they're all kidders,' said Stan. 'Kidding 'emselves ... like tadpoles in a bloody rock pool,' he went on. 'They wouldn't know if they

[21] Tressell R, The Ragged Trousered Philanthropists (Grant Richards, 1914)

wanted a shave or haircut in t' big city.'
   We know though, Stanley. We lived it.

   We are the Ragged …

THE RAKE, 1977

27, THE GREEN
1975

R. PERACH

DRAKE ROAD, 1992

NOTTS. 1992 (DO NOT COMPARE CHESTS
OR NECKS!)

MASTER
OMI

THE
AUTHOR

11

SHOWDOWN

The reality was that our Karate club had been in decline since I'd joined in May '83. It was said that people were working due to the summer season and they'd all be back in the winter, but it never returned to the full strength of the previous years.

Martial arts clubs tend to go through a bell curve of popularity, like most other things. When they start, there is an initial boom of energy and enthusiasm from the new instructor, which is buoyed by the first attendants, publicity and advertising. The interest gets recharged with quarterly gradings, and maintained through progress and achievement, which fosters further publicity, as does success in competitions. All this pushes the club on the upward trend. Around the top end, the club is no longer the new flavour, higher graded students drop out through change of interest, relationships, boredom or satisfied ambition, e.g. if they're happy with a purple belt etc. Then the downward slide begins as the instructor tires of recharging with beginners' courses. Competitions lose their allure and the attendant beginners become faceless, unlike the first batch, who were new and special. The arc takes between two and four years from beginning to end and then it begins again.

Our club had yo-yoed for over a decade and was mid-way on the down slide again. The instructor's brothers, John and Marc, were attending less, Carol had married and left the area and I guess at the time I arrived a few years earlier, I was in the faceless category mentioned above.

Paul had started the club back in 1973, when I was chasing Zara around the playground and playing Planet of the Apes. He was in his mid-20s then, new to the area, having relocated from Sheffield, and only a green belt himself, so he had overseen many re-jigs of the club over the years before I walked in. Also, the aforementioned destructive training methods had led to a debilitating and extremely painful condition in his limbs when he practised, so, after ten years, he stepped aside, and the club carried on as a small group headed up by Bob, who was one of the originals.

Bob was and is an amazing graphic artist. He'd gone on to art college on leaving grammar school in the mid-60s. Fatherhood had come to him very early whilst he was still a student. The handbook for that situation at the time said, 'Get married,' so that's what he and his girlfriend did. He'd graduated and got a job in an agency owned by a lady who probably went to the Weinstein school of HR management. What with that and his beautiful baby daughter back home, he decided to throw it in and retrain in a new profession with his dad's company. There wasn't much call for graphic designers in town back then. Bob's sizeable talent and ambition was outweighed by his heart. He wanted to be there. He wasn't going to let his daughter be dadless.

The changes at our club coincided with a new man in town who would begin his own bell curve. A tough man from a large Sheffield family of even harder men, Mel was the real deal. A Shotokan[22] 4th

---

[22] Shotokan - The most popular style of Karate worldwide, formed by Gichen Funakoshi as the first modern form of

Dan, Japanese trained and graded, he was also a former international and had a big personality.

Shortly before Paul stepped down, Mel had visited us with a mutual acquaintance, and saw we were clearly at the end of our life cycle. He started his club with a boom, and it had all the attendant factors listed above. His training was strong and strict, short of the ignorance and total brutality of the other club but not as warm or friendly as ours. I realised over the years that a certain number of people will pay to be hard by association and gravitate to this kind of training and these personalities. It achieves nothing; it's in their mind but maybe that's all that matters; they're paying to feel good after all.

I'd watch Mel's sessions on occasions and there was no doubting his skills, knowledge and pedigree. Once, in conversation, I mentioned Morris's Karate-do Manual and what it meant to me, even though it was written by a Shotokan man, but he was dismissive of Morris and anyone else of note that I mentioned, letting out a sarcastic laugh.

As Mel's club was booming on its upward curve, I considered defecting, as we were on our knees and I didn't have regular black belt instruction, but I loved everything about our style and our people. It was about gaining something on a deeper level than just personal progress or gratification. This outlook was ingrained in me in all things, a side benefit of being dadless. I've been caught out by mis-placed loyalty often over the years, but not on this occasion. I stuck with the courage of my convictions and stayed put. Comments had also begun to filter back that Mel had been less than complimentary about us and, hearing

---

Japanese Karate-do adapted from the Okinawan original. Shoto was Funikoshi's pen name and Kan means house.

firsthand his disrespect of those much higher in the pecking order, it wasn't hard to believe. I certainly couldn't follow this man and look myself in the eye. So, what to do?

Mel was also a nightclub doorman and not shy about using his fists. He once made the mistake of punching a guy who took too long to finish his drink at, quite literally, kicking-out time. Mel bust his eye, dragged him along face- down by his feet and threw him down the fire escape. The victim, who was a decorator, turned up to work at the client's house the next day with a shiner and carpet burns on his chest and face. The client wasn't too happy; he owned the night club and was Mel's employer. I know because I was there on the job too and it was my mate that copped it.

We'd kept up our training with Bob at the church hall in a very basic sense: combination drills, kata[23], pad work, circuit training and some sparring. It was advertised that there was to be a competition organised by Mel, the East Coast Open, at the Festival Pavilion, Skegness's concert venue. (It was virtually destroyed a couple of years later by the sheer volume level of a Motorhead gig. Pleasure Dome raves finally finished the job.) The upcoming competition would be attended by clubs from Lincoln, Sheffield and the surrounding areas.

A lad called Par had begun to train with us. He was a close friend of Math's and became one to me too. Par was of African heritage, but born and bred in Ealing, in West London. Circumstances had led to he and his brothers being taken in by the wonderful Mr & Mrs Young, who'd moved to Chapel St Leonard's,

---

[23] Kata - a historical pattern of combined linked techniques in various stances, which are sequenced defences and counter attacks in multiple directions.

and were serial foster parents. An entire wall of their home was covered with photographs of all the kids they'd helped over the years; it was like looking at a real version of the old Coke Christmas advert's I'd Like to Teach the World to Sing.

Par was a trainee accountant, successful athlete and a motor cyclist also. He was 6'3" of solid muscle and confidence. Par would collect me for training on his motor bike, and I'd hang on for dear life riding pillion, as we weaved through traffic on the way to the club. Through strength of personality he and his brothers encountered little or no 'race trouble on arrival in the town, because, I believe, they displayed no vulnerability. If something or someone crossed them, they'd meet whatever it was head on.

They were from London, after all, confident and charismatic, with a story to tell, so people wanted to know them and be with them, especially girls. Par was a yellow belt by then and me a brown. We decided we'd enter Mel's competition and Bob did some sport-emphasised training with us. Paul even came back to help for a few sessions, as he did on occasions whenever we needed him. Specifically, he gave me some one-to-one training in the week before my 1st dan grading years later.

Once the competition started, Par seemed to walk through his opponents in the individual events. A born winner, he soon had a trophy in his hand, despite never having competed before. In my category, I did average against a black belt from Lincoln, preceded by a big taekwondo fellow, but got two warnings, both for excessive contact. The Lincoln guy soon put me back in my place, dropping me with a body punch, which was a regular occurrence when I competed. 'Hello again, Mr Floor, how have you been?' I was eliminated.

Par and I were asked by a friendly chap from out of town if we'd like to join him and his pals and form a team. We could enter on the day without pre-registration. Why not?

The draw took place and guess who we were up against? Mel's Shotokan club. Normally, each team's members draw numbers and you'd be up against the corresponding one e.g. 1-1, 2-2 etc. Our two teams knelt opposite each other across the mat, but when the referee went back to the table with his back turned, we rearranged, with Mel and I eager to face each other. This was it. Showdown.

Par and I had been training hard for the competition and as an individual it had been four years since I walked into the Shukokai dojo. I had very little experience of the sport side of Karate partly due to the club's decline, but also because of our geographic location. Skegness was, and is, two hours from anywhere. In hot spots like Sheffield or Manchester, there were in excess of thirty clubs running, so there would be competitions of various sizes happening every other weekend within half-an-hour's travel; experience could be gained within a short space of time. When I was a purple belt, a couple of years before, I'd seen a competition advertised in Combat Magazine. It was at a place called Stoke-on-Trent, which I'd never heard of before. I asked Bob if we could go. He thought about it and agreed. We set off early on the Sunday and as we pulled into Stoke in the early morning it seemed like Pepperland[24] laid waste, from the animated Beatles' Yellow Submarine movie. It was grey, leaden and industrial compared to

---

[24] From the Beatles animated film, The Yellow Submarine: Pepperland, an artistic psychedelic idyll that exists in another dimension only accessible in the eponymous craft. It is invaded and turned silent and grey by the Blue Meanies.

anything else I'd seen. Which was not a lot: an occasional visit to West Yorkshire, and London once or twice on Hogg's day trip coach. We located the sports hall and went to register. I got changed and immediately started warming up. Big mistake. Experienced Karate competitors know that they will be called to fight at 2-3pm. They get changed at quarter to, do a little warm up, then go on and win.

The time came for kata, which I enjoyed and did my current favourite, Ananko, with massive kiais. This got one of the big instructor's attention. I'd recognised him when we entered the sports hall as he'd featured in Combat Magazine: it was Tommy Kwan. He was a Shukokai man too. The judges weren't impressed with my kata though and I wasn't called back. Hey-ho.

Next, it was the individual kumite (free fighting). I was drawn against a black guy, a six-footer, who was a similar age to me, 16 or 17, with a Grace Jones, flat-top haircut. His team all wore red gis, signifying that they were some kind of all-styles semi-contact group. I was all charged up when we stood in yoi (the ready position) waiting for hajime (the referee's order to begin). I dead-eyed him with a fixed, unblinking stare. He raised his eyebrows, a bit nonplussed, and gave a little shrug.

'Hajime!' called the referee, drawing his hands to together and stepping back.

We were off. We closed the distance. I tried a couple of things of no consequence, but with the same 'marmite'[25] kiai that had drawn Kwan Sensei in but turned off the kata judges.

'No more messing,' the guy must have thought.

---

[25] Marmite - a savoury yeast-based spread, the taste of which people either love or hate with equal passion.

In he came like lightening. A reverse punch to the left rib cage like a telegraph pole potting a snooker ball. Diaphragm paralysed; legs switched off. I'm down.

'Yame!' called the referee, stopping the action.

It didn't say anything about this in the brochure, I thought.

There's no count. It's Karate not boxing. In no time, I'm up again.

There was no malice in the guy, but he meant business and all my dead-eyeing and shouting was just broadcasting that I was a very inexperienced lad, with a diet of church hall Karate and Combat Magazine.

His expression was like Michael Caine's put down line from the movie Get Carter:

'You're (not) a big man, and you're in bad shape. For me, it's a full-time job.'

We're going back and forth now, but there's nothing significant from either of us. I get a warning for going out of the area.

Time was called, and I was eliminated.

We bowed and shook hands. He went over to his red gi-ed comrades.

I joined Bob, who was as supportive as ever.

'After the knock down and you were jumping in with the crescent kicks, he didn't know what to do. A bit more time and you'd have got it,' he consoled, somewhat unconvincingly.

I got changed and we watched the rest of the tournament unfold, kids, adults and the rest of the teams. The medics were getting called every second to tend to crying children with angry parents. Bob was quiet and pensive. It was the look of disillusion.

Bob had started in Karate in '73; he'd been to the big event at Leicester when Master Tani (our founder), Mr Kimura (his charismatic leading pupil), and a delegation of Japanese Sensei[26] Suzuki, Omi, Okubo and Tomiyama had given training and demonstrations. He'd also been at the club years later, when Sensei Tomiyama had visited every six weeks. Needless to say, our instructor Paul had trained us all steadfastly in the required principles of etiquette, respect and consideration. We couldn't see much of this in the sports hall in Stoke. Just discipline, no control, lots of rows and calls of 'Mediiiiiiiic!' Just a big mish-mash. It was bloody horrible really.

'Have you seen enough?' asked Bob. 'Shall we go?'

'Yes,' I said. 'It's been good to see it though.'

Like Mr Benn's saved memento at the end of an adventure, my bruised ribs would help me remember.

I went back to Stoke years later. The cartoon Beatles must have visited because it was vastly improved.

The next time we were at the club, we were de-briefed on Operation Stoke by the few members that remained. Bob rationalised what we'd seen, in relation to our ideals. It was, he said., 'A bit commercial ... more the European approach.' This was a kind and diplomatic summary, typical of Bob, and itself preserving the principles we had been taught by our instructor.

So far, the day hadn't been as wild and bloody as the Stoke competition, but this is it. The main event. The Lincoln man had woken me up earlier and I was confident in my reflexes and mobility, if not in my ability to make an impression on Mel physically, as I was all of 19 years of age.

It's clear Mel will try and take my head off, I thought. I know what's coming and I'm ready.

---

[26] Sensei - teacher/instructor

'Hajime!' And we're off!

The referee is Steve Cohen from Lincoln: a big tough cookie in his own right and an old Shukokai hand. It just sprang to mind that the biggie I fought earlier was one of his people. That explains why he was smiling when he took me to one side for the excessive contact warning, 'I know your feelings are running high.' He laughed. 'But calm down, OK?' My poor ribs reminded me again that a lack of control has its own karmic return.

Mel and I closed the distance carefully. Mel had a leery smile fixed on his face. I'd expected an on-rushing steam roller kind of attack and was on my toes, ready to side-step. This guy is much too wily to start that way, I thought, and he's got an audience. What happened next surprised me a little, due to my naïveté and a lack of genuine experience beyond free sparring in the confines of the club. We were a similar height but Mel, as a full-grown man, had a lot of upper body strength; his big Popeye-like forearms were the giveaway. The other thing to watch out for is strength in the thigh, or big legs: the roots of power. One of the hall marks of the Shotokan style is the deep exaggerated stances that appear impractical for real fighting. Another illusion. This kind of training, month on month, year on year, produces explosive attacks, often launched with the weight deep on the rear leg, as I was just about to find out.

Mel edged forward in back stance, still smiling. I stood my ground in my kamae (fighting stance). Aggression got the better of him and he launched, exploding forward, but he stepped right through as I slid out of range, his punch swinging into thin air. He was now stood side on, right side forward. He laughed, mildly embarrassed, as I danced side to side. The referee gestured to continue. I moved back into range. Bang! He'd launched again, and this time connected on the side of my jaw. No score. Too wild, no zanshin[27]. He'd exploited my split-second loss of concentration as he'd attempted with the first lunge, but this time successfully.

I was momentarily stunned from the impact of his punch.

Now it's time for the steamroller.

He surges forward with combinations, but he's missing, even with a leg sweep. I'm back-peddling in a straight line and as I cross the area line -

'Yame!' calls the referee, but Mel doesn't stop.

I lose my footing and he follows me down outside the area as cameras flash. Satisfied with the photo opportunity, he laughs and thumps me on the shoulder.

We both go back to our starting lines. All this has occurred in seconds. We now fight on for a long two and half minutes - attacks, blocks, sidesteps, counter attacks, feints; this is a mental and physical game of chess. Mel surges forward again in a blur but my weight is changing. I step back in sync with Mel's oncoming momentum.

(Bruce Lee, Enter the Dragon: 'As my opponent contracts I expand. As my opponent expands, I contract.')

Yang/Ju/Soft yields to Ying/Go/Hard. All my weight is on my left standing leg and he's still coming. The edge of my right foot finds itself buried dead centre of Mel's broad, doorman's, chest. He is stopped in his tracks by the side kick but appears unhurt.

'Yame!' the referee calls and gestures us to stop.

---

[27] Required composure and awareness following a successful technique.

We go back to our lines.

It should be an ippon.[28]

Mel's smile has gone. We are both looking at Steve, the referee, who is on his mark, feet together, and looking straight ahead between us, as we await his judgement.

Several futures present themselves to all three of us in this brief moment:

1. The referee awards the point. Mel goes bonkers and tries to take my head off when we resume, which he is more than capable of doing. He succeeds, I'm stretchered out and everyone is upset.

2. The referee awards the point. Mel is unable to score, or take my head off in the time remaining, but I'll be dealt with sooner or later by Mel and his colleagues when I'm out in TC's nightclub, where he works on the door. Probably when I'm pissed.

3. The referee doesn't award the point. We fight on until time is called. It's Mel's day. He's who he is. I've given a good account of myself and defended the honour of the club ('Mozzarella or gorgonzola, sir/madam?'), hopefully win Mel's respect in with the bargain and nobody gets hurt, now or later in TC's, to the soundtrack of DJ Bogey.

Future number 3 it is, (thank Christ). No point was awarded to me (due to no kiai and not enough zanshin apparently). Time is called, it's Mel's decision as I went out of the area when he tried to steamroller me for his photo op. We bowed, mine a little deeper, then shook hands and went back to the kneeling positions and watched the remaining fights. Mel's mocking leer didn't instantly return; he seemed to be lost in thought. I looked round and found Bob and

---

[28] A full point achieved with a technique that would effectively end a real fight.

his wife in the audience. He was understated and calm as usual, but now it was his turn to smile.

12

SHADWELL DOGZ

T hat was the name of our band. You can bagsy it, if you like, for your band, because that wasn't *really* what we were called. If it was, you might have heard of us, because it's got a certain ring to it, if you don't mind me saying. But I just thought of it right now along with the logo: Shadwell Dogz in red-sprayed graffiti on a brick wall with a nice paint run streaking down off the bottom of the 'z.' Like from the movie The Warriors. Add that to your bagsy as well.

Me and Dave Mac (AKA Mad Dog) had the most unattractive, repellent name for our band in the history of rock 'n' roll. I won't contaminate your mind by telling you, but it did in fact end in Dogs.

There were three of us: me, Dave and our drum machine, Loose Eel.

I sang and played bass, attempting to be a combination of the bloke from Iron Maiden and Mick Karn from Japan. Dave played a Fender Strat and only sang when he was really angry. He had that many effects on his guitar that he made Kevin Shields from My Bloody Valentine sound like George Formby. We had a range of goth band covers to get going but then, as we were both writers, we knocked our own stuff up.

I'd met Dave some years before. He was in a band with Rob from school along with Lee. Lee and Dave were ex-Big City lads from Sheffield and Nottingham respectively and they'd both ended up in Noddy Town at the Lumley School, a couple of years above Rob and me. They'd been challenged by bullies on arrival, but they'd faced them down and held their own.

Dave recalled to me how he'd been surrounded by a group of wrong 'uns from Ingoldmells at the back gate after school. They were gearing up to give him a group kicking. His dad was close by and intervened along the lines of:

'You want to fight him? OK, you can. Right here and now. He'll fight all of you. One on one and one at a time.'

The scumbags stood off. His dad reiterated, 'One on one! One at a time, today, NOW! Who's first?' They backed off and showed their true colours, which remained the same as when they fancied four versus one: various shades of yellow. They didn't bother Dave again.

The first I heard that Rob and Lee were in a band together was the resultant-piss taking from the twins at school. Rob had made the mistake of letting on that they were called Savoir Faire. That was asking for it really.

Even the frilliest, most make-up-covered, bouffanted new romantic band on the planet wouldn't have chosen Savoir Faire as a name. The twins heard it as Shamwar and were highly amused.

'Shamwaaaar, Shamwaaaar, ha ha ha. Oi, Shamwaaaar,' they'd call to Rob and Lee on sight. Harmless but annoying.

On the last day before the summer breakup, Rob had a tape player on the school field, I was drawn in because the music sounded oriental, and I was Karate-mad at that point. The cassette was Japan's album, Tin

Drum. I remembered seeing the hit song Ghosts on Top of the Pops and how unusual it was. I wanted to know all about it.

That was the start really. I'd got to know Lee as he worked on the boating lake over the summer and we'd talk about music often. He also played me stuff on his Walkman. Over the next year, I worked my way through Japan's albums, one at a time, digesting the content, then a couple of months later getting the next one. There was a lot of progression. I got a shock when I heard their first stuff though, it was bloody horrible.

By now they'd actually broken up. Lee had left school and Rob and I were now 4th years. He invited me to come and see the band rehearse at the back of his mum's house. That's when I first met Dave. He looked like John Lennon, with reddish curtain hair and round specs. He was a bit spiky and acerbic like Lennon too, but this offset Rob and Lee who even at that point were going down the 'nice' Duran Duran road.

The set-up was impressive. Rob seemed to have banks of synthesisers and those things weren't cheap. He was kitted out like any band you'd see on Top of the Pops. My mum had a fund put by, which she'd saved since I was small, so I could attend school trips and things, but I'd never wanted to go. I asked her if I could buy one of Rob's synthesisers with it and she agreed. I now had a Jen monophonic synth. I enjoyed it, but it was a bit of a chocolate teapot really as you couldn't play chords, but I could pick out tunes, so it was a start.

With my boating lake money, I went to Boston on the train and bought a bass. I could now pick out bass lines on that, the first being Mick Karn's outro on Swing by Japan and Peter Hook's Blue Monday, which I played at the request of Lee when we practised.

Rob had got with Priya by then. Jammy sod. Is it derogatory to say she was something else? Well, she was, so there: Danger. High Voltage!

Priya was vivacious, bright, confident and self-possessed. I could go on. She looked like an Asian 'into the groove' era Madonna and was a year older than us. She was streetwise and experienced, naughty but nice.

Priya and later, Priya and Rob, took a lot of verbal crap from a couple of jackals in my circle. But Priya was anti-fragile, it was like water off a duck's back; she genuinely didn't give a damn, or seemed not to. I never discussed it with her, but I should have.

I felt guilty at the time for not intervening and still do now, to some extent. If it appeared to hurt her, I'd have been in like a flash, but day to day, the fire had gone out, I'd renounced violence. It was really down to Rob to step up, but he just wasn't made that way.

Should it have been Priya and me? Possibly, you can tell I was impressed, but that would have taken bottle, wouldn't it? I didn't have any, or not enough at any rate. Maybe like those jackals, I was a little intimidated by this sensual girl. Also, I didn't have hair like Duran Duran's John Taylor and Rob did.

By 1986, we'd been a year out of school. I gave a loving home to a foundling black Westone fretless bass, purchased from Rob, and he had some fresh news; they had a new drummer and singer, also he, Dave and Lee were going into the studio in Nottingham. Dave had written the songs, which were very good, and he'd also come up with a band name: Alice.

They did their demos and a gig was booked at the Richmond, a club set in the grounds of a caravan site.

The singer got pissed before he went on and lost the plot. He shredded his voice and crawled around on his knees in front of assembled friends, family and the general public. Alice didn't survive the night.

A year or so later, Rob got in touch again. They had yet another singer, who was much more compatible, a new guitarist instead of Dave and they were using a drum machine. Would I like to come around for a listen? Sure.

It was 1987 now and they had a set of synth heavy covers, Save a Prayer, Feels Like Heaven, stuff like that, and had been offered a residency at Harrison's ice rink. The band could also rehearse for free, at full volume, in the basement below. I had an original song called I See Red, which we'd done a live recording of, back in the day.

Rob and Lee asked if I'd like to sing it, with them backing me as a guest spot. It was very kind of them, and I agreed. On the night, I had a long dust coat borrowed from Rob and came on mid-point through their set. We had three minutes and smashed it. I was off, and it was in the local paper.

The following week, Rob and Lee asked to speak to me alone. Their new guitarist and singer weren't happy. The word was that my guest spot was the high point of the night, and that if I was given backing by Rob and Lee again, they'd quit.

It wasn't a blow to me. I appreciated them giving me a touch of limelight and we'd been friends for years by then. It must have been good if the others were rattled, but I said I understood. I made plans for solo stuff but, in reality, I was nowhere near ready. I wished Rob and Lee well and watched from a distance. They got on with their residency, did a couple of their own tunes and then went to college to learn sound engineering; they just melted away after that.

Prior to them leaving, Dave Mac contacted me to see if I fancied buying his fretless bass, a similar model to my black one but a much higher spec: walnut body, brass fittings etc. I took it away to try but soon handed it back; it wasn't for me, a bit too luxurious.

Dave then revealed a manifesto. He was so far ahead of the curve as a music lover and an individual with loads of ideas and he suggested we start a band.

Dave was peeved by Rob and Lee's perceived success (I didn't class playing Through the Barricades every Thursday night at Harrison's as success). They were famous on a local level, and it smarted, as they'd done it without him. I didn't see it that way. After all, they'd given me five minutes of fame and let me down gently. Dave wanted to put on a show to prove he could do it too. That was his main motivation, getting back at the others. It was for their benefit.

We decided to go to Reading Festival and see the Mission headline. He had bought a car, an old white Escort estate, but there was one problem: he hadn't yet passed his driving test, so muggins here was the nominated co-driver. I was up for that, but we misunderstood the highway laws, so avoided the A1M and drove all the way to Reading on B roads; it took about nine hours.

We got parked up and into the arena at dusk. There was a crescent moon and the classic Waterboys song came over the tannoy, which was a bit of a moment. As the Cure were also playing, goths were quite thick on the ground. I'd never seen so many alternative people in one place before. It was an eye-opener, as was Glastonbury '90 a few years later. Another key initiation, again thanks to Dave, but on another level completely.

Dave's day job was a ground worker. He was

earning well, compared to myself as a painter, and rarely let me buy a round when we drank together, which was often and usually his preferred tipple, Snake Bite (lager and cider).

Musically, I learnt a lot due to Dave's selected covers, stuff like Bowie's Moon Age Day Dream, Jesus and Mary Chain's Happy When it Rains and Neil Young's Like a Hurricane.

We fizzled out as a band that time, but Dave met Caroline at a party out of the blue and they got married shortly after. I was the best man. I did a little unrehearsed speech saying that I didn't really know anything about love, relationships, or getting married but looking at Dave and Caroline, through to the old folks, I had a bit more of an idea.

Caroline was an art teacher and years later I can appreciate how rich they were culturally as individuals and as a couple. Not in an annoying, arty farty way, just for the sheer love of it. They had all Dylan's stuff, Bowie's, Tom Waits, Van Morrison, the Velvets, you name it. They cooked nice food and read books too. In comparison, I had five Japan albums, Eric van Lustbader's novel The Ninja and some old Northern Soul 45s. Their flat was a nice place to be, but they had a problem. The landlord. He wanted them out, and fast.

Dave explained he was meeting the landlord with his dad at the flat and would I come along as a third party, for moral support and as a witness to what was done and said. No problem. As requested, I stayed in the background and said nothing. The shyster landlord was wary, and Dave's dad played a blinder.

He was in a suit and tie and was a tall and impressive man anyway, a class act. With cool calm professionalism, he tied the landlord in knots. Despite all the upset, the landlord did Dave and his wife an unintended favour. They got a house out of town in the countryside after that and never looked back.

We'd tried to make a band before with another lad called Boogie, a strong and gentle soul and a real individual, his own man. He was 19 like me and even lived with his older girlfriend. Jammy sod.

Boogie and I drove to Lincoln one Saturday and bought drum machines, though choosing different models. Ours was a Yamaha, which we named Loose Eel. Boogie's machine, which he christened Betty, was a Korg.

Boogie linked up with a theatrical punk, Sean, and became The Betty Campbell Experience. They were the real deal as a product. Both pint-sized and seeming to have it all; they looked great, had great rock/comedy songs, personality and were funny too. They even had a comic about their exploits on sale at the Emporium, the underground record exchange near the cop shop.

The Betty Campbell Experience had a proper manager for a while too, and I thought they were certain to smash it, because everybody liked them. Sadly and suddenly, their manager passed away, then they fell out and that was that.

What of the Dogs? We wrote some stuff, did some gigs at TCs, from which we landed our own Bez-style occasional dancer, Johnny Seduction. He was a southern mod who looked like a gene-splice of The Who's Pete Townsend and Nana Mouskouri.

The Marine and Boston's Indian Queen were added to our tiny gig circuit, but unlike the Betty Campbell Experience we weren't really a product. The planets weren't in line for us; they were scattered around the cosmos like the Big Bang.

Dave was always threatening to quit; it felt like it was Let it Be and I was being cast as McCartney: all thumbs up optimistic and organising, and Dave, as usual, cast himself as Lennon: acerbic, awkward, sarcastic and wanting out. Loose Eel was George and Ringo combined in a little black box.

Dave told me before our last gig that he didn't want to do it anymore. At least he'd said it at last, though sadly not to me first. I was gutted because I liked what we did but it was a strain, like any relationship if someone's always wanting something else.

This is bands, folks!

Dave and Caroline went on to have a lovely family and he re-educated as a specialist youth worker, doing an excellent job supporting the Travelling community in and around the Nottingham area. Years later, I saw him on telly in the crowd at a Notts County vs Man City FA cup match with his son, who was the image of him. He didn't look a day older. I messed about for a few years and tinkered with songs. Then lost myself in training, took the road to Samarkand, fell in and out of love and put my guitar away.

But … like Jurassic Park, something survived …

I have a final confession. Our drum machine wasn't really called Loose Eel. You can bagsy that too, if you like.

13

CHANGESNOWONYX

A *Design for Life.* The track's luscious strings and break-up lyrics pulsed from my car stereo as I drove through the dawn mist across the Wolds. It seemed like the Manics could have written that song for us, word for word, line for line. Our journey as a couple was over. It had lasted 18 months but all things are relative, and as you've probably gathered, my journeys tend to be a little intense. We'd met at a party when she was with someone else, but we instantly hit it off.

She worked at a corner shop, near where I trained on a Sunday, and I began to look forward to seeing her afterwards, just for the laugh. Stella was a tall, slim brown-eyed blonde. She was noisy too with a West Country accent and loud dirty laugh like Sid James on helium. Sometime after, she'd become free and single and had got her own place, a little terraced cottage in Alford. She'd called just before I set off for Glastonbury '94 and we'd met up and got along with no skullduggery, as I was unattached also.

As far as my love life was concerned, it was all just rolls in the hay up to that point. I was too intense or too insecure. Always too something or other for a proper relationship, until I got with Stella.

I brought back presents for her from Glasto, a lantern of coloured glass and a Green Man for her cottage. We had a great summer. I did anyway, for me it was the best ever. As the leaves fell for autumn, she got wriggly, after all she'd not long come out of a long-termer, and now she had independence and her own place. Although we seemed well-suited, was she getting boxed in too soon? Reaching out to me was her exercising her freedom, not looking for a real boyfriend.

She wanted out. Or me out, to be more exact. It hit me hard, very hard. I'd been able to let my guard down and express my feelings in a relationship at last. When your guard is down, and your partner's guard is up, just like boxing, odds on, you'll find yourself on your arse and I soon did, emotionally anyway. I was out for the count.

Shortly after, we got back together and picked up where we left off. Booze was at the centre of all we did though. Every night, without fail, we'd do a bottle of wine in. When we weren't at home clacking bottles of wine, we were in a pub drinking or in a club, off our faces.

My stomach often said, 'No!' and sent me to my knees in front of the cold, white altar of the toilet bowl. My innards were made of silk not iron. It was the same with other 'pastimes.' In a flash, I'd be curled up on the floor like Mr Bean in the land of nod. Zzzzzzzzzzz. Too much, and that would be me finished for that night, and feeling rough as a badger's armpit for a couple of days after. Not very rock 'n' roll. Don't tell anyone, will you? Sadly, this wasn't the case with Stella. On and on she'd go, until she was totally paralytic. She'd wake next day a bit bleary-eyed but no headache, no hangover, all smiles.

At first, it's written discreetly in the corners of your life in pencil: 'drink problem,' then it's over all the walls, from the hip, sprayed in aerosol in big, red, block capitals: 'ALCOHOLISM.'

But we were young, we were free, kept our teeth nice and clean.

We were both fit, thought our bodies could cope and, 'Drinking's what you do, innit? Cigarettes and Alcohol alcohol and all that.' We used to drink at a hotel close to home and a member of staff quipped the following day, no harm intended, about how I'd scooped Stella up, so matter-of-factly, at the end of the night, and staggered off home, 'another day at the office' style. Like it's normal.

Christ, I thought, we've got that bad.

Next it was my turn to want out. The whole thing had become painful, but again we talked and got it back on.

In Russian roulette, to raise the stakes and lower the odds of survival, the player adds bullets to the gun following each spin of the barrel. Couples ramp things up to the next level by shacking up, getting married, having babies or buying houses, in no particular order. I bought a small new-build house for us in Louth. That was the next move, out of her cottage and into our new house. We'd agreed that I'd support us until her new business was established. Stella had always been a dancer and natural performer; she'd gone to the Italia Conte stage school and was a classmate of super model-to-be Naomi Campbell. She was now a personal trainer/fitness instructor and was damn good at it. An aerobics class of 30 wasn't a problem - just another kind of performance.

Soon after we moved to the new house, the silliness started again. I knew about all Stella's commitment issues off-by-heart by then. In truth, I was also struggling with the financial responsibilities and was a miserable pain in the arse (my default setting). I caught a glimpse of an imagined future:

more of the same, and in it our kid would be mumless and that wasn't the future I wanted. Not if I'd seen it coming, and I thought I had.

We'd had a blast. The good times were very good. Brit Pop was the soundtrack; we'd even gone to Glastonbury '95 together; she was on my shoulders for Pulp when they played Common People on the Pyramid Stage.

I packed my stuff and went to stay at Mum's, like boys do if the option is available. Stella could stay until she sorted herself out. She'd spoken about going back to her parents in Bristol and making a new start. When she'd vacated, I planned to rent the place out then get my own pad. I didn't want to go back there and be haunted by the ghost of us.

As it was, she soon hooked up with a local bloke nearby. I met them as a couple a few years later on the saddest ever day, the funeral of my dear friends, Andrew Walker and his brother Alex. Stella looked well, and we quickly buried the hatchet. To some degree, it was like the old times, the good times, which was strange on such a day. Seeing her with someone else left me feeling like a ghost, if that's possible, but it was maybe a good sign that we'd both moved on as we should. I shook hands with her new fella; there was no edge. He was big, strong, handsome and uncomplicated, a good upgrade from her ex! The wake rolled on to a pub in Horncastle. I didn't say goodbye when I left; I've never been good at those. I did a night porter and just slipped away...

It was a unique feeling on an emotional level when I went back to Skegness after the breakup. I now had confidence, experience and, at 27, youth was on my side also. My heart was charged with a strange adrenaline. It was the intermingled pain of the inevitable end of a life-changing relationship, and the excitement of freedom with all that the future promised. I felt very bitter deep down for a long time, despite enjoying my escape from responsibility as, in my dumb-ass little mind, I'd laid it all on and committed. I loved her. What more could a girl want? A grown up 'man' probably and I couldn't see further than my own nose.

I now know that something was very wrong deep down on an emotional level as well as the drink issue. Time has told me that just because there's no physical violence it doesn't mean that a relationship isn't abusive. If it hurts all the time, it can't be right. The self-perceived love of one partner somehow can't reach the other, especially if the other doesn't want it.

If someone is determined to drown and not shouting for help, for whatever reason, your first instinct is to try and save them (if you can swim). It's what makes us human, even the worst of us. But they've pressed the self-destruct button instead of self-help, your intervention has flipped into self-sacrifice to an un-noble cause. You will not be Tarzan or Lara Croft, just the other body fished out the water.

I hope Stella found and pressed the other button in the end.

I was now in the age group where my partners were mothers and divorcees and, again, it took me years to appreciate the difficulties these women faced. It was usually ongoing problems with the ex-husbands and fathers of their kids: steroids, cocaine, violence, absenteeism, coercion, eating disorders - take your pick.

I was just candy to alleviate the pain, how could it be more? The ties were too strong and you're always peripheral. If she drops her guard and takes you in, meet the kids and all that, you'll realise it and away you'll go; more pain and tears.

I was told by one girlfriend that we should enjoy each other, but no more than that. She'd assessed the risks and what was at stake. If I had a chip shop, rich parents or owned a caravan site, it could be different. Hard economics, transactional, but this is a material world is it not? Connections can appear unexpectedly on an intimate and very personal level; you wake up suddenly and … (You won't find Billy Ocean in my record collection, but he knows his stuff where relationships are concerned.) Mutual gratification has become love making, with joy comes risk, and the risk becomes too great. She has skin in the game, not you, with your one eye on the door at all times. So, walk through it and keep walking, Mr Icararus.

Eighteen months of all this lad mag hedonism and I was feeling it. We all were. Knebworth was the high point or low point, depending on your perspective, but I was still ascending. Born Slippy, Firestarter, Supernova. But what goes up must … come … down.

Re-entry:

Blow out on damper 3!
Pitch is gone-
Can't maintain altitude!
Oscar, I can't hold her!
SHE'S BREAKING UP,
SHE—
CRASH!

Like the fictional astronaut, Colonel Steve Austin, I'd had a bit of a rough landing and needed rebuilding too. The annoying little pup that had been yapping around my legs since adolescence had become a big black dog: depression. Mild, not, 'I cannae get oota ma bed!' Trainspotting style, but still like having a head full of treacle.

PG Tips, a dollop of Radio 4 and a few early

nights were the bones that would see the dog off for the time being, but it would always be back. Up and down, up and down, like a bloody yo-yo.

I'd had a right bubble (bubble bath: laugh), but something deeper was in order, some love, some beauty.

Back in the summer of 1984, when I peddled to and from my Karate lessons at Winthorpe, it was David Sylvian's Brilliant Trees album that was glued to my turntable, not Wham, Scritti Polliti or any other Radio 1/Smash Hits fodder. It meant a lot to one 15-year-old listener anyway. Sylvian has often been shunned as a vain and pretentious artist by the press, but clearly his notable collaborators, such as Holger Czukay, Sakamoto, Jon Hassle and Danny Thompson, didn't think so. The music was beautiful and evocative, out of its time not of it.

The purveyors this time were a recently reformed also-ran band from the shoe-gazing era, whose singer had finally cracked the art of song writing. Their planets were in line, the world was listening, and the music spoke to my emotions perfectly. They were The Verve and the album was Urban Hymns. Soulful heartfelt lyrics of love and loss, a cosmic star-sailing outlook with a spirituality to boot. The lyrics referenced William Blake and JMW Turner. It ticked all my boxes, and was brilliantly recorded with spectral guitars, rock solid bottom-end and lush strings. It soothed my pain and that of many others.

My emotions were getting pent up again without outlet. Relief of casual sex and promiscuity resulted in more heartache. In reality, free love (always) hurts (someone). It was hurting me. Everything was. Expression through Karate had been key in the past; it had sustained me, saved me and would always be a part of me but I wasn't feeling it now. No personal relationship was forthcoming. I had an eye on the exit door all right, that for me was A1M down to the capital.

I was inspired. If Richard Ashcroft could express such soul and emotion through words and music, then maybe that could be my outlet too. I picked up the guitar again, which I hadn't touched since The Dogs, and did just that. For the next few years, that's where the pain went. Northern Light, Lady Moon, Pod & Pea and Angel of the North, all written on an acoustic guitar in my flat on Algitha Road.

I upgraded my recording set-up and demoed the tunes. The lads heard what I was up to and one of them, Banksy (not the artist), let on that he was a big music lover beyond raving. He brought round stacks of publications from the era, Select, Loaded, NME, Q and the rest. When I finally did escape the black hole-like pull of gravity and move to London, I dropped all these off for Alex at Rivendell. He was 13 then and particularly impressed with the attributes of glamour model Jo Guest and co.

Like the Grand National horse race, when a movement begins, gets media support and catches the public imagination, all starters are off together and indistinguishable, but soon the front runners will break free from the pack and leave the others in their wake. In truth, it's often the ones with the most professional backroom set-up, that control the image, strategy, exposure and everything else; desire + design. In this race, the front runners that broke away were Oasis. The other half of the barbell, Blur, were in actual fact old hands who'd been on a major label for four years previous. Maybe that's why Oasis beat them on the energy and aggression front because they were new and, of course, 'Mad for it.'

Their success story has been well-documented

and has passed into legend, so I won't rehash it but, in truth, luck, timing and a perfect storm of conditions equalling their planets, stars, solar systems and all known and unknown galaxies being in line, elevated them into the stratosphere, along with their talent, ambition and, of course, a stack of great songs.

Their Burnage and my Tennyson Green weren't twinned, but I saw them as kin on a tribal level. They were truly working class, with little education beyond their record collection and off a council estate, as was I. Some might say they went too far sometimes, but they didn't care; they owned the world - maybe that was part of their appeal. They were impervious. No vulnerability on show.

We liked the same things, things that already existed: the Beatles, the Roses, Clarks Originals, Adidas Samba, nice guitars, modish haircuts, anoraks and Man City (everyone's second favourite team until the money landed). The package of look and the tribe existed in advance. Entry level modernism. They didn't invent it, they amplified it. Massively. It was just clever marketing really and I certainly bought it.

Naïveté and romance go hand in hand, and I decided I would, as quoted by Jules in Pulp Fiction, 'Walk the earth like Caine from Kung Fu.' I'd metaphorically tie myself to the mast in the storm like JMW Turner had and as advocated by Richard Ashcroft. I had no attachments. It had to be done. I had four believers. The four musketeers: me (of course), Mum (naturally), Math and Andrew Walker. All disparate and unconnected but they all said do it, so that was it.

I'd read that membership of the Musicians' Union entitled you to free consultation with any of their listed lawyers. A big, kind man from the MU called Nigel McKune gave me time and advice that would serve me well for years. Next, I booked a day of meetings in London just before Christmas '97, interspersed with unsolicited visits to Creation Records and Independiente, the new label of the guy that had signed the La's, Andy MacDonald.

I'd never been to the famous Camden Town but had my trusty A-Z street map of the capital. I came out the tube at Chalk Farm and walked the short distance to Creation. There were a couple of people hanging around outside, an arsey girl who up and downed me, and a lad in original Wallabees with the flowers and slightly raised heel; journalists, I guessed.

The door was open. In I went. Sat at the top of the stairs, squeezed in behind a class-room desk, was Mr Green, the co-owner of Creation. His famous partner was in rehab in his own Northern Light [29] at this point.

'Can I help you, mate?' he said, unblinking while drumming his fingers on the desk.

'Err, yeah … I've brought you this.' I reached into my bag and handed him the tape. He didn't move, so I put it on the desk. He rested his finger-drumming hand on the cassette.

Is he playing high stakes poker with the invisible man, I asked myself. Or has he had Special K for breakfast?

'Cheers,' he said, staying stock still.

'Nice one,' I replied and turned to leave.

Three steps down I stopped and looked back. He hadn't moved a muscle.

'All the way from Skeg, mate,' I added.

'Mm?' hummed Mr Green. One eyebrow went down, the other went up.

---

[29] Northern Light, song about hedonism and breakdown. Way of the Stone - Andy Onyx CD album

'Skegness…Skeggy, you know?' I continued as I descended three more steps. "Get into it, it'll blow your mind."

'Hmm…' Mr Green frowned.

'Blow your mind, mate … change your life,' I said, 'Ohhh yesss.' Then stumbled into a pile on a sticky carpet. I'd ran out of steps.

'Guaranteed, mate, guaranteed,' I shouted up the stairs as I got back to my feet. Then I was out through the door that could lead to adventures. Back on Regents Park Road in the company of the scowly girl and her friend.

Mr Green was what, in the world of espionage, is known as a 'grey man,' probably the ultimate. He wouldn't be seen in a Glimmer Girl adventure. Thick-set, goatee beard and dark curtain hair, you wouldn't notice him behind you in the queue, standing on a train, or sitting in a bar.

Little did I know at the time, but he was originally from Boston, which is the little port town on the road to Skegness, hence the raised eyebrow. Over ten years before, he'd started an indie label with his mate for a laugh. He now found himself at the helm of Britain's most successful record company with the biggest band for years, and many significant others, such as Primal Scream and the Super Furry Animals. Their main act was so popular that they had a label within a label to look after them, which later became Big Brother. So, you can understand the reticence when a Herbert like me shows up at the door, mistakenly left open, unannounced. What did I expect, jelly and ice cream? I had stood before a rock 'n' roll Buddha with 'You shall not pass!' written all over his face.

At Independiente I asked for the A&R who had sent a rejection letter in response to a previous demo.

It was handwritten and said that they didn't like the voice.

Out she came and duly took the tape. A week later, I received another letter. 'We still don't like the voice.'

The MU lawyer's list meetings I went to next had been, so far, inconsequential. Non-starters. The last one was set for 3pm at Cavendish Street. Should I bother? I thought. Yeah, sod it, why not.

There I sat in the reception, looking at all the gold discs and CDs on the wall. They were all significant current acts: Radiohead, Pulp, Oasis. Hello! These guys are for real, I thought.

The receptionist was nice; she asked where I'd travelled from while I waited.

'Saffron Walden, in Essex,' I said. 'Just temporary, like.'

She said she was from Billericay and that was in Essex too.

Out came The Monj and took me to his office, which was in the basement. A very casual, but hip space. We sat opposite each other on leather sofas. The receptionist brought in two cups of tea. The cups and saucers were terracotta-coloured, thick and heavy. The sort you see in Habitat. Expensive.

The Monj leant back and up and downed me much as the girl outside Creation had an hour earlier. Am I flying low or what? I thought.

'So, what do you want us to do?' he said, in a cynical manner.

I explained that I was a songwriter, and The Onyx was the project name. I was hoping to build a team and the lawyer was to be the key member. He raised his considerable eyebrows. 'Suppose we'd better have a listen to it then,' he said and went and put it in the stereo. He sat back down and switched it on with the remote.

Freekin' Ada! I thought. Northern Light, written and recorded by a painter from Skegness in a flat on Algitha Road, is now playing in the office of a heavyweight music lawyer in the middle of London. The audacity, missus. GET IN!

'Hmmm.' The Monj cocked his head to one side 'What else is on here?'

'Two more,' I said. He sniffed and played the first verse and first chorus of the other tracks. 'How much more have you got of this?' he asked, while stroking his ear lobe.

'Loads, about 50 songs,' I lied. 'Written,' I then added.

On the recording, I'd dubbed a descending guitar note after the first line in Northern Light, trying to simulate the slide guitar of B.J. Cole on Urban Hymns and the mellotron swoop on Strawberry Fields. These pearls were lost on him. 'There's no market for country music, this production won't do,' he snorted. 'Acoustic's how we like it, stripped down, very basic. Just like The Drugs Don't Work … even I can play it.'

Well, I haven't been thrown out and we're on a conversational level, I thought.

'How do you feel about input?' asked The Monjinator.

I let him roast for a few seconds of silence.

'I'm down with that,' I said. 'You guys are the experts, you know what will sell.' All what he wanted to hear. His eyes lit up, but I couldn't make out if it was because he wanted fingers in the pie on a creative level or the 'ker-ching!' of pound signs.

'Well, go away and do some more, strip it back and get it back in to me,' he said, reverting back to semi-dismissive. 'We'll pick this up in the new year. Where do you live?'

I explained and said that I would be relocating to London in the new year, sometime soon.

'Of course, you'll need a band, unless you're planning to go out on your own.' He looked down his considerable nose at me. 'Which I very much doubt.'

Well, we'll see about that, Jonathan, I thought to myself. We'll see.

The Monj wanted to keep the tape and an A4 graphic of the Onyx logo I'd had done. I'm not mad or crap, I thought (clearly, I was wrong about one of those). It had got legs. I couldn't wait to get home and talk about it to the other Musketeers.

I was going and going for good. This was not an experiment; I'd got the skills and trade to survive alone in London. I could take care of myself, but it would take careful planning. If it was rushed, I'd be scuttling back to Skeg with my tail between my legs and I wasn't going to let that happen.

I had a job to do for a relative in Saffron Walden. The plan was to wrap up the Algitha Road flat with a month or so to go, stay at the job and use that as a base to scout out a place in London.

A lot of my stuff got binned and I kept the essentials; my whole life had to fit in the back of my Sierra Estate car: guitars, tools, clothes, stereo, and porta studio. The hope generated from the meeting with The Monj sustained me over the next few months. It was nothing but something at the same time, a breeze that lifts a spark to a flame. I did as he said and re-recorded Northern Light and the other tracks and sent them over. In between life, I'd call him now again; this was way before email was in regular use. He generally said he hadn't heard or listened to it yet. 'I'm not ignoring you,' he'd say, presenting me with a bizarre paradox.

The plan was going well, and the time came to

take the plunge and hand the keys of the flat back. Whilst packing the last bits, a couple of strange things happened. I had the radio on; it was a show celebrating Bowies 50th birthday. It was called changesnowbowie, a skit on his two great compilations changesone and changestwobowie. He was there in the studio, and the format involved the presenter, Mary Ann Hobbs, playing various pre-recorded birthday messages from ephemeral pop stars, in between the interview and music. Bowie, ever the gent, gave polite comment and thanks to the likes of Brett Anderson, the guy from Placebo and Ian McCulloch. All gnomes in Ziggy's garden.

Then one message stopped him in his tracks; it was from Scott Walker. Scott wished him happy birthday and thanked him, saying that the important thing, the thing he commended him for, was that Bowie and his music had freed so many artists. Bowie was speechless for a couple of seconds, even possibly moved for a moment. He then took a breath and said in his South London accent:

'Oh look ... There's God in the window.'[30]

I noticed a free compilation CD from the monthly Q magazine that I'd somehow missed. I unwrapped the cellophane and put it on.

Now, on that CD there were many bands, and in amongst the pack there was a track, and, on that track, there was a bass and, in that bass ... there was something. Something about the bass line on the outro that I couldn't put my finger on. I put it on repeat and listened again and again. I couldn't figure it out, so I let it go, and got on with the business of leaving but the bassline thrummed on in my head.

---

[30] I found out years later that the quote was attributed to the four-year-old William Blake in 1801, the first of the artist's many visions.

We often hear the term 'echoes from the past.' Well, this was an echo from the future. An echo of things yet to come.

The band were Primal Scream and the track was Burning Wheel.

On a sortie into Liverpool Street, I'd got the Evening Standard and checked out the accommodation. I went to an agency in Baker Street; there were two places in Belsize Park, a bed sitter and a studio. The girl advised the studio, as it would be much better for me (more commission, sucker). I went and had a look; it was expensive but secure. I went for it on a short lease, so I could keep an eye out for something cheaper. All paid up, I went back with the keys and moved in.

Primrose Hill was a short walk away. It was just before the August Bank Holiday weekend. I sat there on the grass at the top, looking down on that huge slab of concrete baking in the sun: London. The hard cruel city, Blake's London. As immovable and unforgiving as her sisters: Tokyo, Paris, New York and Berlin.

Bright lights and paved with gold? I was under no illusion. How many have gone down there with a mission and come unstuck over the years? I asked myself. Better men and women than me? Maybe. Well, I've got to go down there and make an impression, shit or bust. The arrow is flying, there's no going back. Ding-ding, seconds out. It's on. Changes now, Onyx. I have a direction; I'm tied to the mast. Bring on the storm.

14

I THINK YOU SHOULD SIT DOWN

I searched online on a semi-regular basis over the next few years, the same way I had on the day of the revelation. By 2005, the results were limited to whatever new information some unwitting soul had uploaded. The latest article stated that my father had joined a Magicians' Guild in Nottingham and they were very happy to have him. The President of the group was a historian of magic, so needed no introduction and was aware of my father's status within the pantheon. He was able to forgo the usual entry requirement of a performance before their committee in leu of a lecture, described as somewhat deep (check!) on the Psychology of Performance. They had also posted that there was to be a show in Nottingham in which he would perform with Paul Daniels, the big in the 80s TV magician, who was topping the bill. I contacted the group to obtain tickets. This was it. I was going up there to put the man on the spot. The resultant handy work of one night in May 1968 would be on the march up the M1 right into his face, like a 5' 11" karmic boomerang. As it comes so it goes. I imagined his attempt to placate and squirm out of the corner I'd penned him into at last, and my response:

'Hey presto! An inconvenient time? Damn right,

cunt!'

The man who allocated the tickets for the show began to get cagier and cagier on the phone, in the end requesting cash to be sent in the post. Maybe I'd let on too much and they figured out I was homing in on the magician for reasons other than my love of rabbits and top hats. As it goes, I had to do some work, shop-fitting in Reykjavik, Iceland, and would return the day before the show. I opted to abort what could have been a very messy meeting of genes.

By 2005, the day had come. I had married and due to Assa, my wife, at last I felt together as a human being. Safe, wanted and loved. Life and tragedy had depleted my Musketeer support group, before I met Assa on a blind date and took it from there.

Our only transactions were love, commitment and a copper engagement ring from H Samuels . A handmade, culture-clash wedding in Paris soon followed. All our friends and family: Malians, Londoners, Parisians, Northerners and an essential Skeggy Town Raver enjoyed our memorable day.

We found ourselves el skinto, like most newlyweds, but there are other kinds of wealth beyond basic needs. We supported each other with little help beyond ourselves to rely on; month by month we stumbled then climbed, fell and climbed again, as we have done to this day. When the bell for the slug fest of life rang from then on, I had the best corner person in the world; we would lose or win together.

I was inside at last and strong enough to deal with whatever would transpire. Assa didn't care if I was a painter, a baker or a candlestick-maker. Being loved and respected for who I was had dulled the bitter edge of being dadless.

A route one confrontation with Papa was now thankfully, well and truly off the menu. I began to have a less toxic and more balanced view, up-grading him from Satan incarnate ... to what though? Having fully talked The Situation, and all anticipated echoes and ripples, through with my new wife, I finally felt I was ready and planned a different approach. I contacted the Magic Circle and asked if they could contact my father on my behalf, not revealing The Situation but that I had information that he may appreciate. I gave them my name, mobile contact number and waited ...

Months later, I was doing some shopfitting work on an evening shift in a bank in Fulham. It was the one and only time I have ever worked through an agency and had taken it on due to my regular company going through the famine end of their feast or famine cycle, and bills needed to be paid. It was around 19.30 and I'd just got started. The phone rang. Number withheld. The caller asked my name and then gave his and stated the line that I'd given the Magic Circle. The voice was calm, deep, polite and seemed well-educated but not affected or upper class, with a slight Jamaican accent. I couldn't have been caught more off-guard.

Now I was collared at an inconvenient time. In nano seconds, I ran through options, angles and possibilities. I couldn't risk asking for a call back. Neither could I risk asking for his number so I could return his call. That would raise suspicions and could close the door, forever. As Eminem said, you only get one shot. So, I talked.

'You can put the phone down at any time and I don't have your number, but I have to ask you some questions, OK?'

'Yes,' he said.

'Were you working the summer season in Skegness in May/June 1968?' I asked.

Pause. 'Yes.'

Deep breath. 'Ok, so I guess you'd better sit down,' I advised.

There was some nervous laughter. 'Really?'

'Yes, are you sitting down?'

More nervous laughter-but shorter. 'I am.'

'There's no easy way of saying this," I said. "It stands to all probability that you are my father. As I said, you can put the phone down at any time, but I'm going to give you a lot of information to verify what I say is true, so you'd better get a pen and paper.'

At this point he trotted out the bollocks that it wasn't possible, as he had an injury at the time etc. Which I then shredded with pure certainty. He stayed on the line, and I gave him the full uncensored dossier marked The Situation, and what transpired in the fallout. He interjected with careful responses throughout and maybe took notes. I finished with an understandable, 'Do you think I could make this up? It couldn't be anyone else.'

He then recounted some of his life in that era and said that he was separated at the time, so any indiscretions didn't count, and chuckled that he had a very special friend. (The word was that my father was rolling around with the coast guard's wife at the time, in full knowledge of the coast guard himself, who was very understanding!) But he said he really couldn't remember anything about it, and couldn't place my mother at all. (I was also told, but didn't recount to him, that the aggrieved party had come down to Skegness in March '69, confronted and 'educated' him regarding the incident nine months earlier).

On our conversation went. He explained that he hadn't been well, that he was a vegetarian-(check-ish!)

and that he couldn't introduce me to his family because of something that was going on at the time.

I explained that I'd been very angry and bitter for most of my life. He said he understood and was sorry that he hadn't been there for me. I explained that I'd enjoyed a lovely upbringing, surrounded with love nonetheless.

We finished with me thanking him for hearing me out, and saying he should look over the information I'd given him and check it out with my blessing. I said that a great weight was off my shoulders now, no matter the outcome. I didn't ask for his number and he said he would call again. He did, twice more.

The second call consisted more of him pressing me on what I did for a living. I explained I was a painter and decorator; he was distinctly unimpressed.

'Do you like magic?' he asked

'Not particularly,' I told him.

'Hmmmm.' He said that he thought he could remember my mother, but then said it was another girl in Kings Lynn. He explained that her parents had put her through university and, 'She'd gone and got herself pregnant.'

All on her own? Quick, call the Vatican! This guy's more Teflon Don than Lounge Lizard, I thought. Anyway, he said he'd call back. He did. Once more.

It was a Saturday morning, and I was at home with Assa. The phone rang, number withheld. This was the third and final call.

'How do you I feel about a DNA test?' he asked. He said he'd been talking to a lawyer he played golf with (of course ... Malcom X would love this 'house' guy) and he'd advised that it would be a wise move.

'Fine,' I said. 'What's involved?'

'I've no idea." He laughed. 'But we're buddies

anyway, no matter what.'

We openly discussed the fact that there are a lot of people out there whose fathers aren't who they think they are; in my case the marker of colour was there for all to see and the culprit clear. Others live in blissful ignorance, with silent doubt or a sneaking suspicion lying under the surface, due to a stunning likeness to the milk man or Uncle Derek. I explained, a little annoyed finally, that I had a great family already, I'd contacted him with noble intentions but wasn't looking for another one.

'We're buddies anyway, no matter what,' he repeated. He didn't call again.

For a couple of years after, I seethed. Had he tried to use his hypnotism on me with the 'buddies' mantra, trying to introduce the element of doubt into my own mind? Was he gaslighting me? Then I got angry. Very angry. Angrier than I'd ever been with anyone. Not just for me. I felt this guy had taken the piss out of all of us, especially Mum, as well as all those damaged by The Situation, who carried the pain for decades after, most of all my real mother, who spent her life coming to terms with it.

I felt it was a truly smack-able offence. If he could be 30 years younger, I felt like I'd happily batter him for his disregard for the pain caused, and sacrifices out of love, by good people, all those who had mopped up after him. If it was us, and the girl in Kings Lynn, how many more? I'd educate him properly for his serial piss-taking, then go and make a cup of tea … but he couldn't be 30 years younger, so I wouldn't be doing any of that.

Two years or so later, I did the same internet search that kicked the thing off. It turned out that he'd died a year or so previously of pancreatic cancer. This must have been the 'thing that was going on' that he had skirted around in the first conversation. I greatly value our three chats, despite how it ended. He didn't need to call me; it took bottle. I believe that he knew what I'd said was true, but that he was ill, and he knew it. There was no way forward, but was he right, were we buddies? We did get along and seemed to have some things in common. He's been described as 'a friend to everybody,' so what can I say? I would have loved to have done the idealised thing that dads, sons and daughters do and go for pint. It would have been great. That will join the list of should have, would have, could haves that we all have tucked away.

If it's still a possibility for you and you never get around to it, no excuses, maybe you should … or maybe not.

But it's your call.

15

NORTHERN/EXPOSED

O n 1st September '98 I woke with a special feeling, safe in the knowledge that I'd finally done it. I'd moved to London. Back in the day, aged 17, working with John I'd said, off-handed, that it's what I'd be doing maybe next year (it had taken me ten) but it had taken a lot of planning and wasn't done on a whim.

A fresh crack at life, with no strings attached, was a lot to ask with even more to gain: to become a new man. A gift like this had come at a cost and a big one at that. To make the proverbial omelette I'd had to break an egg … and the egg was me.

I'd had some flyers printed:

Renaissance Decoration

Estimates Free

Floors sanded and finished

Interior / Exteriors

All wall coverings

I liked the sound of the word 'Renaissance'. I'd heard it often in my circle, as it was the name of a popular Nottingham dance club, frequented by the Skeggie Town Ravers. It sounded posh to me, and I didn't connect it to European cultural movements, although Renaissance was apt, because its literal translation means 'rebirth' and I was at the beginning of mine. I was 28 years old and had been blessed with an entirely new start. No one had been abandoned or let down. I wasn't running away; I was running toward.

I went door to door, posting the flyers in the streets and houses around England's Lane in Belsize Park, where my studio flat was.

I'd seen a group of painters working on an outside on Steeles Road, no, not on Supernova Heights, (the residency of one Mr Gallagher) just an ordinary if large and expensive house. I didn't post the flyer there. Best not take the mick, I thought. So, I dodged that house but took note.

The painters were all relatively clean in decorator's overalls (but not too pristine). They were laughing and joking (harmony is always a good sign), sheets were down, and they seemed to be doing a professional job. I carried on around the surrounding streets, door to door, but later I came back.

Since I'd had to go self-employed to stay with John at 18, I'd had what's called a 714s card. It had an ID photo and was hard to come by. They were issued to sub-contractors by HMRC as tax exemption cards. In short, it meant that you could be paid in gross with no admin, hassle or tax deduction for the hiring party; you just issued them with dockets as receipts. A chancer wouldn't be in possession of one. It also meant there were no ties. For whatever reason, you could be gone at any time. Stan's few serious words to me a decade earlier now took on more gravitas.

I took out my 714s card, presented it with the ID facing outwards, and approached the painters with care:

'Hi, who's in charge?' I asked.

They all turned. A fresh-faced stocky guy, a couple of years older than me, raised his hand.

'Me, I am,' he said. This was Frankie Grabham. One of the owners of Grabham & Twistham, which he ran with his business partner, Peter Twistham.

'Are you looking for a good decorator?' I asked.

Frankie took the card, examined it for a few seconds and compared the ID with my features.

'When can you start?' He smiled.

I was to go to a wall papering job following the Bank Holiday at some offices in Covent Garden. The first big test. Could I hack it in the Big Bad City, with my skills and knowledge and on my own? I was unfamiliar with the paper, a wide vinyl, but Frankie explained how to apply it and it went well. I survived; I was good and quick enough.

I felt a sense of achievement getting to that moment, from starting on the YTS as an art college reject and all that had happened in between. That's the whole point of properly learning a trade. You can rock up in a big city, any city, and exchange those skills for money to live and eat, not because your face fits or who your dad is, but because you can really do it.

I had a secure base and work: a toehold on the sheer rock face of London. My studio room was stark, I just had my stereo and instruments. Purposely no TV. I'd come here for a reason, not to watch Coronation Street, and if I wasn't working, I'd be out and about revelling in my freedom. Soon I'd walk for miles across the city, taking it all in.

It was my first evening in London after a day's work. Naturally, my senses were heightened, as they are in any foreign or unfamiliar place. Everyone else was in their normal routine around me: people, cats, dogs, birds. Business as usual, an ordinary day. But for me it was completely different. I walked into the Washington, the bar on the corner of England's Lane, and ordered a pint. It was quiet. History by the Verve was playing on the jukebox. With its orchestral string arrangement underpinning the track, it had set the template for the band, before they temporarily disintegrated. It also referenced lines from the poem by William Blake: London. The world around me was oblivious, but for me this was a very good omen. The Masterplan by Oasis was on next. I'll take that too, Mr G, I thought and raised my glass unnoticed. In the heavens above the rooftops of NW3, it seemed like my planets were drawing a little bit closer.

I gave The Monj a periodic call over the first three months in London, leaving a message for him with Miss Billericay or, if he did pick up, he still 'hadn't heard it yet.' In the end he reeled off a list of labels whom he said he had submitted the tapes to, and none were enthused, so that was that. The Monj had been instrumental in my decision-making but would not be as crucial to the project as I'd initially hoped. It wasn't a blow as I was here now and living it.

The decomposing horse was flogged a little longer by sending tapes off, to no avail. I took a day off work to go to the MU seminar at Camden Palace. A musician called Obo was there. He was six or seven years my senior and he lived and breathed for jazz. He had also come from Skegness originally and was a close friend of my old neighbour, Russell. He'd pressed and released his own recordings and was asked to sit on the panel with Nigel McKune, who'd given me some invaluable advice a couple of years before. We didn't exchange numbers and I never saw him again, but it was great to meet another who had walked the walk before me.

There were fliers on the table about a Cultural Industries course at South Bank University. I made enquiries and enrolled on a Tuesday evening in St John's Street, Islington. The attendees were generally a little younger than me and included those that actually worked at independent record labels, distributors, lawyers and a couple of people with ambitions like mine.

I presented myself as a songwriter, looking for publishing. They had speakers each week from different areas of the media, such as art dealers, entertainment lawyers, label bosses, and TV producers, who accepted questions at the end. It was all very good value. I learnt a lot and made a couple of significant friendships. Some lasted and others fizzled out, as is the way in London.

One of the fizzlers was a guy called Daz from Preston; he'd been a club promoter up there. Things had got big, lucrative, then dangerous, as dealers and gangsters wanted a piece of the action. Daz also had ghosts to deal with. He was haunted by the promotion experience, which he described as near death, and also with the guilt of abandoning his daughter and her mother. His grand plan was to make an animated version of Aldous Huxley's novel, Brave New World.

Daz kindly gave me a copy of the book which I still own. Tony Blair was PM then and riding high, long before his catastrophic decisions regarding Iraq. He seemed like the embodiment of the book's all-powerful World President, Mustapha Mond, saying: 'Well, you know, everybody's happy nowadays,' in his,

'I'm a kind of straight sort of guy,' mode.

In return for the book, I gave Daz a tape, which he listened to in my presence at his squat in Hackney. Since meeting Obo, I was starting to think about independent recording.

'It's verging on folk,' Daz said, looking mildly perplexed. He then hit me with a hard fact that I could ignore but not evade:

'Have you got a following?' he asked. That was something that hadn't occurred to me. I had a simple answer: 'No.'

'It's no use making records if you haven't got a following,' said Daz. 'You need to play out, then you'll see.'

He was right, it was the only way now. Live performance. I had some cash from a job on the side and went to Macari's on Charing Cross Road. I saw a semi acoustic guitar (one that you can plug in) that I liked and asked to try it. I looked up and saw Andrew Innes from Primal Scream talking to the shop assistant and remembered the Burning Wheel anomaly. I dranged out the Syd Barrett-esque descending riff. He didn't notice, or if he did, he didn't show it or was mildly annoyed.

I left Macari's with my new guitar and practised solo performances to attend floor spots and open mic nights around North London. The main one that fitted into my weekly schedule was at the Lock Tavern, which was between Camden and Chalk Farm and took place in the small function room upstairs. It was devised and hosted by an Australian compere. Apparently, he'd been a regular in the soap opera Neighbours as a child actor. His manner was supercilious and sarcastic; he seemed to take pleasure in cutting the players off or taking side swipes at their performance or material. The compere reserved a spot for himself each week and sang his songs to the captive audience. A fellow called Kenny Connor, who was no mean singer/songwriter himself, described the compere's style as Christian Fellowship, a put-down far more apt than any he laid on others. This guy's who he is, I thought, so this is a good test. I asked him if I could play and he agreed .

The first time I played, I stumbled but got through. After all, it was my own song, 6 is 9, so nobody really knew the difference. I was angry with myself despite this and keen to come back and have another go. My confidence grew over the weeks, and soon I could get through a couple of songs without fluffing it in a room full of strangers.

This is where I met Homblfuyt. He seemed like just another through the revolving door of players with semi acoustic guitars, but he had a very distinctive, rhythmic style of playing and the songs were great. One in particular, The Kingdom of Love, stood out to me but he had lots more. He was slightly aggrieved at the limit of two songs for the floor spot. I found Homblfuyt gregarious and outgoing; he'd offer his hand and introduce himself to anyone, no bother. He was tall and confident with jet black hair, thick eyebrows and piercing brown eyes. He also had the disposition of a March hare and a disarming, mischievous smile, that was somehow reminiscent of Muhammad Ali.

Another character showed up that night, a long-haired Mancunian, who equally had a lot of front. He had distinctive features: blue eyes, an olive complexion and a slightly hooked nose. This was Zaid. He claimed to have been born in Baghdad and to be half-Iraqi but raised in Moss Side. Zaid was looking for acts. He said that he'd ran a floor-spot night for years in Brixton called Zags but had lost the venue. He'd secured a new one at the Blue Post on Newman Street next to the BT Tower and invited everyone down.

Before that, Homblfuyt had given me his number. I rang him, and he told me there was a festival at the weekend that his mates, a band called House of Rhythm, were playing at. I'd gone along; it was fine, and I met few more people. We agreed to meet at Zaid's club the next Thursday. Things were picking up socially. The wilderness era was thankfully coming to an end.

By now, I'd left the studio on England's Lane, and moved to a bedsit in Highgate that was a third of the price with no bills; heating and hot water included. I just had to share the bathroom with 15 other people! Truly clean living in difficult circumstances; hard but cheap.

The bedsit had been advertised in the Ham and High paper along with a couple of others around the area that I'd viewed and found weren't suitable. I'd arranged to meet the landlord at the property one October evening. It was dark when I arrived and there was a welcoming light on in the hallway, visible through the frosted glass. I rang the bell and was greeted at the door by George the landlord. He was middle-aged with a grey Bobby Charlton comb-over and spoke with a German accent. George stood a little shorter than me but was powerfully built. He seemed all upper body, a bit like Fred Flintstone, with little legs carrying him around. George also resembled a chef, with a neckerchief around his neck in white material and some kind of apron on.

He invited me in courteously. The house had a very nice ambience. It was warm and clean with a spicy, pleasant smell of home cooking. This was due to the Filipina housekeeper, Tess, who lived on the ground floor, next to the front door.

George asked if I would excuse him for a moment. There were two young men further down the hallway. They were remonstrating with him about their deposit. George began speaking with them in French, they responded in kind but then reverted back to English, either because George's French was bad, or they'd prefer me, as a prospective tenant, to hear what was being said. This went on for a while but didn't escalate. In the end, George reached into his pocket and pulled out a wad of notes. They came to an agreement and the guys left in peace.

George showed me the two available rooms. The one upstairs was only £60.00 a week but really was a broom cupboard with a sloping ceiling, so I went for the £75.00 one on the ground floor. It had very old furniture and a fold-out sofa bed. There was old lino on the floor of the kitchen section, which comprised a pedestal basin, gas fridge/freezer and cooker. A flaky sash window with yellow curtains looked out onto the rear garden and the backs of the terraced houses on Archway Road. I could almost put the world to rights with my good friend Bill Psyches over there, using light switch Morse Code. There was just about enough room to swing a malnourished kitten.

Eager to impress, I had brought along my college work to show George that I was studying, and also evidence that I too was a landlord and had a property back where I was from. George was enthusiastic. I was the kind of tenant that he wanted. He explained the terms, we signed the contract, and I activated the break clause at England's Lane and moved out. I'd be in that house for the next four years, although for the last one I had a larger room at the front on the first floor. Luxury!

Regarding his rent, George wanted it in cash and

stashed in the same envelope, same place, month on month, year on year. He'd note the collection date then strike that out and add the new one each time (I still have this as a souvenir). Like a fool, I missed the first rent deadline. He was standing there waiting in my bedsit when I got home, but I'd collected the cash and handed it over. He didn't rant, but he wasn't happy though when he left, we shook hands. Instead of letting go, he put a crush on. That old chestnut. So, I reciprocated. We stood in the middle of the room, both smiling, with eyes locked, but with sweat running down our backs, as we put every ounce of our beings, and those of our ancestors, into a mutual hand crush. After what seemed like an eternity George grimaced. 'Danke. I must be going, ja?'

We released our grips.

'OK, George, thank you,' I said.

'And do not forget the date for the rent again, please, Andrew.'

'I won't forget, George.' I tapped my temple twice with my forefinger. 'Don't worry now. Take care.'

'Bye, bye,' he said, and off he popped. My hand went straight into the frozen peas.

Prior to the Lock Tavern and Blue Post, I'd discovered a Sunday acoustic night at the Hope and Anchor in Islington and got to know the promoter long before I played there. It was the first place in London where I could walk in and be acknowledged by name. I could handle my own company and considered myself self-reliant, but a few months all alone in London with no-one to talk to, bar work banter, and you really appreciate those small, human interactions.

I'd go to retro clubs at the Monarch, drink and dance but couldn't really open up. I was, as Bowie said in Ashes to Ashes, a little 'locked in myself.' I'd knock female interest back out of insecurity and knock male friendliness back out of homophobia.

Fear to the left...fear to the right... ohhhh youuuu sad twat.

Getting the boy out of Skeg was one thing, the opposite would take a lot of work ... and time.

At the acoustic nights, it was my language, heart on sleeve, a chance to let off steam a little. As the Blue Post's nights rolled along, Zaid managed to rope in newcomers each week, as did Homblfuyt. As Homblfuyt didn't work in the traditional sense, he'd arrive in central London on a Thursday afternoon and get plotted up with his guitar in Soho Square. His usual chat up line was: 'Hey, do you wanna be in my magazine?' It would change, depending on the girl or the circumstance, to film or video. It was his icebreaker, that's all. He'd make a beeline for anyone with a musical instrument and they'd be invited to his club that evening. He was the catalyst and the Blue Post did indeed become a club of sorts, with regulars, due to its central location.

Homblfuyt was originally from Reading, and he brought along a small circle of friends that had also come to London over the years and made their way but were still close. The Blue Post brought them together again. Some just watched and enjoyed the music, such as Tom and Rachel, but others arrived with instruments and played small sets.

One was a small chap with a Parisian bob/mop-top hair that obscured his eyes. He resembled a young, scaled-down version of Gene Clarke from the Byrds. Modish but individual, his attire showed consideration and a clear attention to detail. He had the chilled-out demeanour of Dylan, not Bob, but the animated rabbit from the Magic Roundabout. This was Mr Janus Street. One night, he brought a genuine Hofner violin bass and played along. He also drove a vintage, silver BMW that looked like a giant zippo lighter. A bit of a geezer, by all accounts. He didn't drink either, which for me was unusual and refreshing, as I was still getting trolleyed on a regular basis.

Mr Street was quiet but sociable. The music did the talking for all of us really. I'd begun to play Northern Light and Lady Moon and the little crowd of regulars had begun to request them, which meant a lot to me.

Everyone had their small set of songs. Street mainly played with Gareth, another of the Reading posse, under the moniker the Gallows Tree Jug Band. He later explained to me that his family had relocated to Reading from Fulham when he was just getting old enough to go on the tube on his own and explore London; this was a blow to him at the time. Reading had seemed slow, almost rural to him on arrival; even the words people used - namely calling plimsoles 'pumps.' Urgh! He'd soon found his feet though, forming and maintaining lasting friendships through a shared love of music. Homblfuyt's band, which he called the Unity Tribe, had an ever-changing ensemble, involving percussionists, various bass players and a flautist. Then there was Stone Valley, a duo you couldn't pigeonhole, made up of a black girl singer, Sharon, backed by a white male guitarist. Boss Man was a solo act, a shy young Welsh guy, who had a different force when he plugged in his guitar and got in front of the mic.

The 11th of August 1999 heralded a rare national event. No, not a Royal Wedding, much rarer, a solar eclipse. There were various commercial festivals down in Cornwall, which would have the best vantage point. They all consisted of entertainment for a couple of days, culminating in the eclipse at midday on the 11th.

Homblfuyt had sourced a grassroots type festival called Sunbloc, probably through the Big Green Gathering connections we'd made. Leanne Bouzouki, another Blue Post regular, would provide the wheels. She would share the driving with me and Boss Man, and Homblfuyt would … er … navigate. We'd agreed to set off following the Blue Post gig on a Thursday night. We arrived at dawn. It was a truly grassroots affair but was still well organised, with familiar faces from other festivals, such as Fergal and Aster. They were a young Irish couple who had created the Piano Bar venue, which had also been at Glastonbury and the Gathering. It was a little amphitheatre, dug out of the soil, and covered over, with a piano and stage at one end, like the Blue Post and then some.

If you played, they gave you drink; the more you played, the more you drank. We all did little sets, along with many others. It was great. The festival had the accompanying merchant stalls that grace most of these kinds of events. While I was playing, I looked the short distance across the amphitheatre. There was a black guy pointing and smiling with a small group. Did he know me? He sure did; it was Barney from my school tutor group, the only other black kid at the Lumley School back then. He had a stall selling festival masks and paraphernalia. There were only 60 or so punters at Sunbloc so I don't think he made much money. Like the circus, he had gone by the next morning and we didn't get a chance to speak, but it was great to see him so far from where we'd met and were from and at such a one-off event.

On the lead up, we went into St Ives and Penzance for a drink and fish and chips and had two days of glorious sunshine. Everyone emerged from their tents on the morning of the 11th to be greeted by a leaden, overcast sky. We all gathered at the predicted time on the cliff edge with loads of percussion, bongos and bells playing. I was stood next to Jerry Dammers and his partner. Day became night for a minute or so.

'Have you seen Homblfuyt?' I asked Jerry.

'Yeah, last night,' he said with a look of mild concern. 'He was over with the pagans, trying to persuade someone to walk the red coal carpet.'

The PA system provided at the Blue Post was no frills, to say the least, and was dubbed the Hamburg by Homblfuyt, after the Beatles' pre-fame residency days.

As the momentum grew, Zaid began promoting the club properly with press adverts in Time Out, The Metro and Bar Fly. In turn, we would be given a headline gig, with the others doing one or two songs as support. Mr Street's band would be the first headliner and it would be on a Saturday as opposed to Thursday. Zaid had invested in a better PA, but he wanted us to pay for it.

'I ain't paying, take it away, I'll settle for the Hamburg,' said Homblfuyt. That was that; it stayed for one night only, and Zaid footed the cost.

When I got there on Saturday, everything was set up and I was just a bystander. For the headline slot, Street's band had been expanded to include a drummer called Magic Dean and a keyboardist, who seemed strangely familiar. The set was great, with off-kilter songs, some countrified or bluesy, others strange-a-delic, like Aquarian Moon. It was a nice night of music in a space not much bigger than your living room (but much bigger than my bedsit). After the set, I found myself stood, shoulder to shoulder, with Street at the bar.

'Your keyboardist looks like Mick Talbot from Style Council,' I said.

'D'you think so? Hmm ... yeah, I guess he does.' He smiled and went to join the lookalike and the rest of the Gallows Tree Jug Band.

An evening Media Law course carried on from the initial one I attended. As an act, I hadn't got a fully-fledged following like a proper band, but the performances were happening, and the feedback was good regarding the songs, so the idea of doing something independently had begun to grow.

The people that ran the course made us aware of the funding that was available and where to get it. There was a business advisory unit near the tarpaulin at Portobello Market. The boss there, Maria, was very kind and helpful but there was no money available. The other thing was the Prince's Youth Business Trust. I had turned 30 by then, but their rules stated up to and including 30 years of age, so I was eligible, but it was no walk in the park. I had to produce a complete business plan for the first (not the last) time. Maria from Portobello was invaluable in supporting me with this. I had never touched a computer before, so the whole thing was typed out with one finger. If the business plan was accepted, I would also have to meet and be interviewed by a panel. There was £3,500 riding on it, and it was only a loan, albeit at a very favourable rate, which had to be paid back over the next two years.

There was also a compulsory meeting with a PR company in Cavendish Street, not far from The Monj's office, where I met other prospective business starters. For the majority of them, the Prince's Youth money was just a little extra, along with the other funds they had raised. For me, it was all there was, and in real terms we had to record, press and promote a product with £3,500. I soon rowed back from this; the money would be spent on demos with a view to getting some kind of development deal.

Mr Street had a house in Twickenham that seemed ideally suited to what little I knew of his personality. A nice layout, and a garden with doves in it, much to the amusement of his friend and occasional tormentor, Homblfuyt.

It now emerged that he had started as a DJ as soon as he was able to return from Reading in his teens. He'd played regularly at Dingwall's and numerous warehouses in the late '80s and been in the final incarnation of Style Council, along with Messrs Weller, Talbot, Lee and White. From there, he had landed a record deal on fellow DJ Gilles Peterson's Talkin' Loud label, amongst the burgeoning acid jazz scene. His band was the Young Disciples and their album, The Road to Freedom, had been pipped to the post at the first ever Mercury Music Prize by Primal Scream's Screamadelica. The award night began a long association between Street and the Scottish band. In the years preceding our meeting, he'd done a lot of notable bass session work. All in all, Mr Street had been on the front line for ten years as a successful DJ, musician, producer and songwriter, with the accompanying indulgences. It had knackered me and I was just a fan, nowhere near the centre of it all. So, he'd gone away for a while to rest, reflect and recalibrate. But Mr Street was re-emerging. The Blue Post thing was almost part of a rehabilitation process, playing for fun with no pressure, with his old friends. One of his last bass sessions before his sabbatical was for Primal Scream's album, Vanishing Point.

It was Burning Wheel.

We were at Street's Twickenham pad for tea and

I explained the whole Prince's Trust scenario to him and Homblfuyt. He kindly hand-wrote a note with a mini resume, saying he rated the tunes and if funded would act as producer. Following a round of interviews with the Trust, which culminated in a meeting with Sir Michael Heron, I, or rather Village Green Recordings[31], was funded. I had a very warm glow walking from the building at 9 Eldon Street, part of the impenetrable slab of concrete I'd viewed from Primrose Hill on my first day a little over a year before.

Homblfuyt now had a new line: 'This is Andy Onyx. Prince Charles has given him some money to make a record.' He was a bit wide of the mark with that one, but it tickled us all, as usual.

Life had become very compartmentalised. Frankie, my boss at work, had been in on what I was up to with music and found it all little too bizarre. With things taking off, I was struggling with timekeeping and energy. Also, he didn't like the eclipse trip; maybe he was jealous of my freedom. His father, Frank Senior, worked with us and was a great character. As with Stan years before, I'd hit it off with another boss's dad. Frank Senior, though an older man, retained a certain athleticism from his youth, as ex-soldiers and former sports people often do. He worked hard and had a great sense of humour. The Royal Irish Rangers were his life as a young man, and he'd been posted to the Belgian Congo in the early '60s. He often told me stories of his exploits: funny ones, not violent or gory stuff. Despite his large family, it seemed that his army

---

[31] Contrary to belief, I chose Village Green as an amalgam of Highgate Village and Tennyson Green, not as a homage to R.D. Davies or The Kinks, although I am a fan (of the music) and still think that God should Save them.

days were his happiest.

The surprising thing was that the family were Jehovah's Witnesses. Frankie and his brothers knew no different; they'd been raised in it. The only separation from ordinary life beyond their beliefs was no sex before marriage, if you were with someone in the faith, and no birthday or Christmas celebrations. As a kid, I'd won the Good News Bible in a school art competition (Samson pushing the temple pillars down) and had read it, so if it did come up in conversation, I was able to discuss things frankly (pardon the pun) and openly. Frank Senior and his wife, both born and raised in Wexford, Ireland, had got to the point that they couldn't reconcile their Christian faith with what they saw as the contradictions and hypocrisy of the old Church. They needed something else and for them the JWs ticked the box.

All the work we did was based on insurance claims, usually water leaks. The customer would have a leak, put a claim in and we'd come and decorate the area. One of the customers was the Hare Krishna temple off Soho Square. We had to redecorate the male ashram (sleeping quarters) and the job was given to me and Frank Senior to do. It was a laugh, as you can imagine. We had to literally throw a sheet over some devotees because they wouldn't move off their bunk beds when we painted the ceiling.

Luckily, Frank Senior had some common ground with one of the senior guys there, Vidura, who was also a big Irishman, ex-military and a former mercenary. Throughout the job, I started having some spiritual conversations with the devotees and found out more about the Beatles' involvement. George Harrison had given them the deposit for the temple there and bought Baktavindanta Manor for them at

Watford.

I returned after we'd finished the job and began attending on a Sunday, the one day of the week when I could have a truly nutritious meal. At one point, I was so thin I hardly cast a shadow. It was acceptance and shelter in a spiritual environment. They asked nothing of me. These people helped sustain me in the hard and lonely life of a newcomer to London. When I sold my house, as a thank you, I returned and re decorated the male ashram entirely. I still visit occasionally now.

After the cardinal sin of time off for Sunbloc, I wasn't the flavour of the month any more with Frankie and Paul and got phased out. My journey with Grabham and Twistham, which had begun with my fortuitous approach on Steeles Road, had come to an end. They'd given me an essential toe-hold on my very first day. Things could have been much more difficult. As Stan told me years before, this is our world, so get used to it. I picked up other work for while then went out to Goa, India, for a month with my old pals, the Skeggie Town Ravers, to see in the new millennium.

We started recording in mid-January 2000. The studio had been found by trial and error and was called, much to Street's and my amusement, Odessa. Our laughter was due to the connotation to the film The Odessa File, based on Frederick Forsyth's book and starring Jon Voight (Angelina Jolie's dad)

From that day to this our phone calls to one another always began with, 'Jawohl!'

The studio was situated in what was then known as the 'murder mile' area of Clapton and set back from the road. You wouldn't know it was there. It was as if it had a TARDIS[32]-like cloaking system. On inspection, Street said the desk, mics and live room compared well to those of Solid Bond, Mr Weller's old studio. Odessa also had an excellent house engineer, Gwyn, who spoke Mr Street's language fluently: ANALOGUE.

As producer, Street called the shots and had selected Pump, Galliano's drummer, and Sir Jimmy Rover (Mick Talbot) on the Hammond B3 organ. Every morning, I'd drive round the north circular to Street's dove garden for 10.00am. We'd psych ourselves up with a breakfast of organic tea and Green & Black's milk chocolate and set off to Odessa in Clapton by 11.30.

We played Street's mix tapes en route. I'd spoil you if I revealed the tunes right now, but I'd never have come across them, as with a lot of the finer things of life, were it not for him.

One cassette I had in the car went down surprisingly well. It had been a Christmas present from my Aunty Margaret when I was about 13. I'd described the cassette case in Woolworths to her: 'Bowie's face side on,' but I couldn't remember the title. What I was hoping for as I ripped off the wrapping paper on Christmas morning 1984 was changesonebowie. What I got was Love You Till Tuesday. As Street and I set off East each morning, we'd be singing along and laughing our heads off in no time. It's no Hunky Dory, and slightly out of focus, but the ingredients for what would become vintage Bowie are all there. Namely imagination, drama and the voice, which was still very Anthony Newley. It's

---

[32] Time machine from BBC TV series Dr Who. TARDIS is an acronym of Time and Relative Dimension in Space and is often used as a general connotation to something that appears to be bigger on the inside.

almost like he's too many things at once and can't decide on an identity. He hasn't yet pulled it all together and decided on a wrapper, which of course he'd done by the era of Ziggy Stardust and many times since.

Dadless, yes, but my world and life absent of Mr David Robert Jones's input/output is unimaginable. What would I have done without him?

All the bones of the tracks were down on day one in live takes; the next two days were over-dubs and mixing. Gwyn, the engineer, often talked about a novel young local band he was helping out on the side. He said they were local kids in their early 20s but had a pensioner drummer, which worked really well, and they would probably pop in at some point.

Every musical instrument can be traced back to the first Stone Age musicians banging bones together, then eventually discovering acoustics with empty gourds, various twines, the introduction of electricity, valves and so on until in 1935 the Hammond Organ was invented. From then until now, nothing sounds quite the same in the right hands, and in Sir Jimmy Rover we certainly had a pair of those, so we hired a Hammond B3 in for him.

The whole thing is a big beast of a set-up with the keyboard, case and Leslie speaker. Mick's parts were soon down, and we were all mesmerised hearing his playing on Lady Moon, clean in the control room. We used software digital keyboards on later recordings, due to budget and convenience, but it was an honour to see the knowledge and experience at play with the B3 under Mick's control. His manipulation of the Leslie speakers speed of revolution and the 'under the bonnet' stuff; all the subtle tones and nuances he'd set on all the analogue switches, pulleys and pedals. Mick's performance stood alone perfectly well without our muted instruments and was joy to be immersed in at volume. We snapped out of it when the singer from Gwyn's little band also showed up. He was very tall with half-mast trousers and had big chunky brogues shoes on like those that the animated Mr Men wore.

'This is Pete,' said Gwynn, 'from the Libertines.'

In three days, we had four tracks finished and mixed. What then?

If Odessa really was a TARDIS, with hindsight, would I have travelled back in time to talk Jazz Man Gerald into releasing a double A side 45 of Angel of the North and Lady Moon on his Stark Reality imprint? That was the advice of my live band lead guitarist and mucker ,Adrian Owusu from the Soul Destroyers (later to become the Heliocentrics), but I didn't follow it.

Gerald had got them moving, along with Little Barrie, with minimal heartache or expense. Like me, Barrie had walked the road himself but from Nottingham in his case, with his drummer and backing vocalist Wayne. He got plotted up with a job in the vintage guitar shop on Dean Street, located an identikit bassist and his planets lined up above him like an astral snooker cue. But that's why time travel's banned: by altering the past, a lot if not all, of the ensuing adventures wouldn't have taken place, due to a vain whim for instant gratification and success, and you wouldn't be reading this right now. So, here's to reality!

As for the Odessa sessions, I was thrilled with the recordings. We'd also had a laugh and the feedback was generally positive. It was back to the ragged reality of construction for me though. I'd got the trip for millennium in Goa, a tax bill and George's bedsit rent to pay. I didn't fancy another shake hands session.

After all the activity and ascent of the previous year, topped by the Odessa recordings, things plateaued. Time was wasted hawking the recordings around labels again. The backdrop to this was the disintegration of the record industry due to Napster and the 'dot com' boom. As ever, a few bands and artists were still being signed though, but on much more spartan 'one album' deals.

A trusted friend's manager said she wanted in. I had reservations because she didn't present any plan, never mind an impressive one. Also, my friend had already landed the original deal off his own back but selected the manager at her own insistence. This manager wasn't a Simon Napier Bell (Yard Birds, T Rex, Japan), Tony de Fries (Bowie) or J&L Dickens (Adele), who would invest time, money and faith in their charges to get things moving.

If this manager didn't truly inspire me, then how seriously did the people at the labels take her? On reflection, maybe music biz managers have their specialisms, just like their equivalents in football, e.g. keeping a side up, gaining promotion or silverware, and hers just wasn't landing deals. She wasn't that daft though, because she still had muggins here doing leg work, duplicating and dropping off CDRs at her office after a day's work. After months of messing, she told me that she'd like to publish Lady Moon herself. I said I'd think it over ...

One of the semi-regular attendees at the Blue Post was Tony a singer/songwriter/producer from Ladbroke Grove. He knew I was struggling. He introduced me to Ross, who was a DJ and A&R man at Island Universal. He'd been given his own Island Blue imprint by Chris Blackwell to develop cutting-edge new acts, but his free hand had been taken away by the merger with Universal and the writing was on the wall. He could, however, still facilitate studio time. He booked me in at the Island Studios for a couple of days. The personnel were the same, bar Gareth, who came and did backing vocals, and the house engineer, Steve, who was equally talented on the digital side as Gwynn was on analogue.

Four more songs down, no contract, the fax machine was jammed. The best tune was Dig, which we all concurred was the best Christmas number 1 that never was. Probably a John Lewis Christmas ad smash in a parallel universe for someone (it may yet be in this one). At Island Universal, they had their weekly A&R playback meeting and Ross informed me that there were no takers; I was free to go.

At the first meeting, Ross gave me a compilation he'd put out off the back of his Radio London show, Destination-In. It had a standout track, Sugarman. I asked him about it and the singer, Sixto Rodriguez. He said he was from South Africa, his sister was over there, and she'd made him aware of Sixto's album, Cold Fact. 'Nobody knows anymore,' he said. 'It's very underground, there's little else ...'

I'd sold my house at Louth and was able to square up debts, including paying Mr Street a day rate for his invaluable help on the Odessa recordings. Mick wouldn't take any money, so, following Street's advice, I got him a couple of records: The Meters and Mose Allison. I also offered to paint his house too, but he wouldn't have it.

You often hear talk that a particular celebrity or famous person is really down to earth, because they maybe had the good grace to say please or thank you to a nobody like you or me. This man, from the moment I thought he was a doppleganger in the Blue

Post, exuded quality, class and also measured force. Many young bands and artists have been lucky to enjoy Mick's moral and creative support over the years. He was present during the recording of the Young Disciples' Road to Freedom, back in the day, helping crystallise the band's youthful talent and energy in a big studio environment.

People who've had a brush with fame often puff themselves up, but I found Mick self-depreciating. Once, when being interviewed by Robert Elms on BBC Radio London he explained that after being a pop star in a pop group' you have to ask yourself if you're a musician, not a pompous serious musician, just a musician. And if you are, providing the music's right, you play, that's it, period - as our American friends would say. Mick was being characteristically modest regarding Style Council; they were much more than just a pop group, as their back catalogue will attest and posterity will one day recognise.

In one week, he played live gigs with Burt Bacharach at the Albert Hall, the Gallows Tree Jug band at the Blue Posts and Ocean Colour Scene at the Forum, all great gigs but I wonder which he enjoyed the most. Mick also taught me that it's not just about haircuts, shoes and music. Art, film, and especially books and reading, are just a big a part of it. He turned me on to Colin McGuiness, starting with City of Spades. Get into the range, he'd say, it's all out there, that was the whole point (no pun intended): Full Spectrum Modernism.

Mick could also straighten out any bad behaviour in his air space too. Any rock 'n' roll antics (silliness and immaturity) would be frozen out with a steely blue-eyed stare. A couple of seconds caught in the Merton laser beam and I'd get the message and be back in line! A last word on Mr Talbot: back in 1985, whilst still a Style Councillor, he didn't arrive to play Live Aid at Wembley in a Colombian helicopter or on a magic carpet, as did some other stars, he plumped for buses and trains like most of the audience. Incidentally, that coincided with me being on the YTS at Stepney and Son's in Skegness, at the mercy of people bereft of the qualities I've mentioned above.

Street and I joked, looking forward, that when the pay dirt hit, I'd get him a green Morgan sports car, so he could tear around South West London like something from Wind in the Willows. My debt to him still stands. He seemed to take to anything quirky and unusual; luckily that included me. As you have probably gathered, I take great stock in the 'master and apprentice' relationship. Ours was along those lines, which he would laugh off with mild embarrassment, but he was certainly my mentor. He genuinely liked my tunes in their own context, but I think the fact that there's this mixed-race guy, out on limb, unhinged, in a bedsit and he's working to pay for it, struck a chord. Very unusual. Maybe.

We once met on the street in Notting Hill in my tea break, as I was on a site nearby at Blenheim Crescent. Naturally, I was in my white overalls, and a bit sweaty and dusty. He related this to Pete Townsend who once had a similar stage get-up in The Who. The Skegness factor also amused him.

One day I got a call:
'Jawohl!'
'Jawohl! What's up, Mr Street?'
'Yeah Onyx, it's about Norman, guess what?'
'Norman? Norman who, Norman Wisdom?'
'No, Norman Jay, guess where he's playing?'
'You've got me, go on...'
'SKEGNESS!'
Peals of laughter. Marvellous. Norman Jay MBE,

Good Times superstar DJ, mod and cultural icon and the spiritual leader of Notting Hill Carnival, had been booked to grace a venue in Skegness, by someone with impeccable taste and deep pockets.

I'd managed to get a sale or return distribution deal for Ignition through Cargo at Parsons Green, again due to Mick being on board; he opened the door. Craig, the account manager, was a big Style Council fan. Mr Street and I took a load of concept art images and psychedelic posters and printed them; our designer Auto was a mutual friend of Matt Julian, a fellow student from the college course. He came up with a classic design (as he did I on the other releases) and Ignition was pressed and released. (Cue tumbleweed.) Followed by a 45' and a 12". (More tumbleweed.)

Ernie from Galliano took up my offer of work on his house in return for use of his studio, Boogieback, on Colney Hatch Lane. I just had to pay Nick the engineer. There was no Mr Street this time, only his work on the Odessa and Island recordings. He'd recorded an album's worth of high-quality demos with the Gallows Tree Jug Band and things were hotting up. A multi- millionaire rock star had started his own record label; the demo had been playing on rotation in his band's tour bus and he had his eye on Gallows Tree Jug Band, or on their music at least …

In the Boogieback sessions, Ernie played bass, Mr Owusu did lead guitar and we also had combined horns: sax from Jacko Peake, who'd played flute on both Mr Weller's solo debut and Wildwood albums, and trumpet from Achilleas, a magnificent young Greek who did live work with The Soul Destroyers and the Dandy Warhols. These recordings became

Way of the Stone, the final Village Green Recordings release. It is the only album on the planet with this line-up, including vocals from Australian humpback whales. I try to keep abreast of what my collaborators are up to as I'm first and foremost a fan. Hopefully, those whales are still singing their beautiful songs today, deep below Hervey Bay on the other side of the world.

In June 2004, Andy Onyx's Way of the Stone hit the shelves, a fag packet Hunky Dory. Then the shelves hit back. (You are now passing through Tumbleweedville, please drive carefully)

The great original rapper and self-defined bluesologist, Gil Scott-Heron, prescribed the music of John Coltrane and Billie Holiday to get you through a rough spot. I'm down with that, but I also consider Gilles Peterson's BBC 6 show sonic and spiritual nutrition; whatever's going down, the tunes and guests will get you feeling better. No agenda, just sit back, open your ears and let it happen. He recently had On-U Sound's legendary record producer, Adrian Sherwood, as the special guest. When interviewed, Adrian attributed a quote to Island's Chris Blackwell, regarding some releases that were still born and ended up much nearer the earth's core than the intended underground audience: 'Without promotion something terrible happens ... Nothing!'

Mr Blackwell probably used it in Mr Sherwood's presence, and no doubt on many other occasions because it seems unarguable, in relation to going to market with any product you're hoping to sell.

The quote's originator was in fact the legendary showman PT Barnum, and its strength doesn't redeem Barnum from being, possibly, the biggest bullshitter known to man. Why? Because it's not true.

Well, not entirely. Something always happens, but that something, sadly, without the platform of exposure, may not be a crucial sales target being reached in the next quarter, saving your job, house or marriage.

This right now is something, is it not?

If you own it, you can break it. A life lived is a story to be told, especially if it's true. CDs become MP3s and digipacks recycle as great mosaic art, CDs become a teardrop mobile installation.

The signed original of 'Mr St*rwood said,' digipacks on canvas is a nice piece, if you're into that sort of thing.

16

THE END IS WHERE WE BEGIN

Writing and sharing these stories of my journey with you has meant a lot to me. I hope we've had some laughs and other stuff together on this little trip and I wish you well.

I've naturally carried all the events around for the duration, but the catalyst of putting pen to paper was this: in the course of business, I had a new client, I'll call Pablo, a young black man of mixed heritage. He is smart, well-educated and good looking (jammy sod) and is a qualified surveyor, and now a businessman with a burgeoning, diverse, family company. Not dadless.

Inspiring. A great change. Things are going his way.

At first, I felt kinship with this young star, then I reflected. Was I fooling myself? What had my world to do with his, apart from our ethnicity? Maybe something, everything or most possibly nothing. I'm 13 years older and was born in a different circumstance and era, in a vastly different Britain. I held the thought but stopped the comparisons right there. Is this not the way it should be for Pablo and anyone else having a go out there?

Around this time, I also received Grayson Perry's

book The Descent of Man[33] as a Christmas gift from my sister. I'd seen his Brexit programme, where he interviewed both sides, even sharing cab journeys with ardent 'leavers' in Boston, Lincolnshire (near Skegness). Clare, his alter ego, would probably have proved too great a distraction and wisely stayed at home that night, averting a Benny Hill chase around the docks. I'd said that, all things considered, I thought Grayson Perry had balls of steel. Reading the book later was like a Damascene revelation, as it put masculinity itself in the dock and held a mirror up to fifty per cent of the world's population, daring us blokes to take good look at ourselves. I rose to Grayson's challenge, looked in the mirror and reached back. I recovered my own story stashed away in the back of my mind and examined the behaviours, the battles, the adventures, the disappointments and the triumphs.

In the foreword of this book, I used the term anti-fragile for myself as, for me, disadvantage became advantage and most setbacks became opportunities. But what of the others? Those stranded on the shore with their souls kicked in, who couldn't fight back? The ones that aren't made that way. Disregarded, written-off and forgotten. Is the Britain that they're living in so different, like Pablo's, or much closer to mine?

At the time of writing, in the British Isles last week there have been approximately 84 young men, whom we can firmly establish were not anti-fragile. They chose a different fate; that of our old English teacher, Mr James Love. There were 336 male suicides in the last month and 4,000 in the last year. Add young women making the same tragic choice and the figure

---

[33] Perry G, The Descent of Man (Penguin, 2016)

increases by a third.

If they aren't legion, then I don't know what is. Talking and listening would be a start that is needed. Is the young psyche of the nation being forced into a corner by combined snapping predators, too many to list? Bitten and stung, accused and demoralised, via a smart phone? Every generation has its challenges, which are usually lost on the one that came before. Where I'm standing, it looks rough in places for the youth of today, with reality as endangered as the environment, but they will crack the code. Connectivity can also provide positive friendship, kindness and support from behind that glass too, pointing back to the human factor.

Most of the lyrical content of Marvin Gaye's classic What's Going On? resonates more with what I see around me as each year goes by, just delete the Vietnam War and fill in the blank. I'd never heard it until the year 2000. It was playing in Honest John's on Portobello Road when I walked in. It was love at first hear, and we left together shortly after, straight back to mine. It lifts me from the speakers like a spiritual life raft, whenever I hit a brick wall, get a head full of treacle and find that black dog having fun on my leg.

Off the rope
The butterfly float
Goliath fall
Badness smote

Maybe I'm familiar with some of your setbacks, maybe not, but I chose 'dadless' as the title for this book and not 'Brick Walls-Up Close and Personal: 1969-2018', or 'Hope - Between Bob and No', because once I started, it went beyond that defining void in my life, spotlighting the revolving cast of characters who filled it over and again, with time, inspiration, humour and ... OK, let's say it, love, when I needed it most.

What do some of the other totem-like giants I've leant on in times of trouble have in common: Muhammad Ali, David Bowie, Bruce Lee, William Blake, Robert Tressell, Arthur Dooley (look him up), Grayson Perry and the Beatles? Certainly not their tailors; could you imagine them together, Stella Street revisited? All the unusual suspects were working class outsiders, with a total dedication to their work and an appreciation of the beauty in life that surrounds us. They also balanced the torture of such immersion with humour and fun whenever possible (an essential bubble, now and then). Did they have sherbets on their shoulders too? Maybe. All were written off at one time or another, before confounding their detractors and hitting their peak, though sadly in Blake's and Tressell's case, not in their own lifetime. Their 'best bits' are part of my self-prescribed solution to the black dog, along with lots of talking, walking and good relations at home, the occasional beer with a trusted friend and my own output. Everybody needs some self-expression. Including you ... yes, you. So, get to it.

I now find myself in the championship rounds of life. Still fighting, game and reaching out, but I know I've been blessed and lucky too. After all, you're reading this.

Coming back to the question my father asked me when we spoke for the first time, 'Do you like magic?' Years on, maybe I can say I do, and I've been amongst plenty of it, after all. Not his abracadabra stuff, or surface repairs I do to make ends meet, but the real magic, the kind that surrounds all of us when we're not looking. The stuff that fills the space between free will and kindness and makes good things happen as if by …

But, if I could, I'd to like to ask you one last thing.

You can take it how you want, and I may not know you from Adam, Eve or anything in between.

I also know it's not as simple as it sounds. Far from it.

Just one final request?

If I could ask one thing?

I'd ask you to live.

§

SOUNDTRACK BY CHAPTER

THE SITUATION

Hey Jude – Wilson Pickett

Whitey on The Moon – Gil Scott Heron

TENNYSON GREEN FOREVER

Chirpy Chirpy Cheep Cheep – Middle of the Road

A Windmill in Old Amsterdam – Ronnie Hilton

Hushabye Mountain – Stacey Kent

KUNG FU AND CLANGERS

The Tra-La-La Song – The Banana Splits

Sweet Gingerbread Man – The Mike

Curb – Congregation

Rebel Rebel – David Bowie

AN ACT OF ABJECT COWARDICE

Too Much Too Young – The Specials

Metal – Gary Numan

Mary's Boy Child – Boney M

FROM VIOLENCE WITH LOVE

Visage – Fade to Grey

James Coit – Black Power

Sensitive Mind – General Assembly

HELLO, MR LEE

Let's Dance – David Bowie

Is There Something I Should Know – Duran Duran

Billie Jean – Michael Jackson

WAY TO THE WAY

Ink in the Well – David Sylvian

I'm Free – The Soup Dragons

World in Motion – New Order

THE LAKE

Grease - Frankie Vali – Motion Picture Soundtrack

Love Action – The Human League

The Look of Love – ABC

WE ARE THE RAGGED/ SHOWDOWN

Walls Come Tumblin' Down – The Style Council

West End Girls – The Pet Shop Boys

Stepping Razor – Peter Tosh

SHADWELL DOGZ

My New Career – Japan

Happy When it Rains – The Jesus and Mary Chain

Moon Age Daydream – David Bowie

CHANGESNOWONYX

A Design for Life – The Manic Street Preachers

Burning Wheel – Primal Scream

Rumble in the Jungle – The Fugees

I THINK YOU SHOULD SIT DOWN...

How Can we Hang on to Dream? – Tim Hardin

Big Louise – Scott Walker

Fire in My Heart – Super Furry Animals

NORTHERN/EXPOSED

History – The Verve

Plastic Man – The Kinks

Let Me Sleep Beside You – David Bowie

40,000 Headmen – Traffic

THE END IS WHERE WE BEGIN

What's Going On? – Marvin Gaye

I am the Black Gold of the Sun – Rotary Connection

Move on Up – Curtis Mayfield

dadless Spotify Playlist:

https://open.spotify.com/user/49r61oipn4da
de6v1tj3biom6/playlist/7gdChdqIrHlalMwOSA
7ajm?si=KvCdZsIsT3OC2X_MuTeASg

ACKNOWLEDGMENTS

My stone felt thanks go to anyone over this half century who provided this stranger with a hand of friendship, ears to listen, time to read, back to feed, a warm embrace or a wing for shelter.

Particularly those 'set on repeat' at the London end, most notably Tom Williams, Bill Psyches, Mr Janus Street, Sir Jimmy Rover, Brendan Conroy, Robert Woodland, Dave Marvin, Secret Moona and Paul McGoran.

Kerry Hudson's Breakthrough, which pushed me over the line.

My editor, *The* Debi Alper.

Most of all my wife, Assa, my black gold of the sun. Without all she has given out of love, I may never have gotten over stuff, cracked the code, or even survived. Tied to a man/child, in turns sad, bad and completely mad, she got me better and finally walking tall. There really aren't the words x.

ABOUT THE AUTHOR

Andy Onyx was born in West Yorkshire in 1969 and grew up in Skegness, Lincolnshire.

He has lived, amongst other things, as a painter, martial artist, musician and educator. He is married and has enjoyed adventures in London and beyond since 1998.

Other books include the BARBELL series of Spy Fiction Novels, *The Glimmer Girl* and *Shamstone*.

@AndyOnyx1 | andyonyx.co.uk

Printed in Great Britain
by Amazon